Noble Drew Ali Plenipotentiaries
And the Negro, Black, Coloured Addiction

Written by
G.S. Bro. Kudjo Adwo El

Edited by
Sis. Tauheedah S. Najee-Ullah El

2nd Edition

©2014, 2020

I0379750

Moorish American Prayer

Allah
Father of the Universe,
Father of Love, Truth, Peace, Freedom and Justice
Allah is my Protection, My Guide and my Salvation
By Day and by Night,
Through Her Holy Prophet
Noble Drew Ali,
AMENRA ASE ISLAM

Contents

King Alfred Excerpt	Page 1
Edward Mealy El	Page 4
Prophet Cherry	Page 17
Sweet Daddy Grace	Page 19
Father Divine (George Baker)	Page 20
Elijah Poole Bey	Page 22
Marcus Garvey	Page 28
Duse Muhammad Ali	Page 36
Nigger Addiction Withdrawal	Page 40
Martin Luther King Jr.	Page 42
Muhammad Ali	Page 54
Ernesto Che Guevara	Page 58
General Khalid Muhammad	Page 61
Yasiin Bey	Page 62
Jeff Fort	Page 65
Visual Alchemy	Page 68
Bibliography	Page 72

King Alfred Plan, Executive order #11490 or code name "REX-84" is a contingency military plan, an executive order of ridding the United States of America and the World, FINALLY, of the MINORITY, all black, negro, coloured, Hispanics and poor whites. This document was first drafted in the 1960's then revitalized in the 1970's by the hand of President Jimmy Carter and finally revised by president Ronald Regan in 1984. This executive order was declassified several years ago which means it is NO LONGER affective. This means that there is an ALTERNATE PLAN or REVISED PLAN in place now.

The executive order of REX-84 called for the following:
- The use of hand pick African/Hispanic leaders (especially religious leadership);
- The use of military basis as prisons;
- Militant groups (Caucasian) to be deputized to assist police forces;
- The use of Military forces to assist in gathering minority people;
- All Black leaders to be detained;
- All Black Senate and Government officials to be detained;
- All Black Military personal to be disarmed and detained;
- All "Sympathizers" to be detained.

Combined Memo:
Department of Justice Preliminary Memo: Federal Bureau of Investigation & Central Intelligence Agency.

There are 12 major Minority organizations and all are familiar to the 22 million. Dossiers have been compiled on the leaders of the organizations, and can be studied in Washington. The material contained in many of the dossiers, and our threat to reveal that material, has considerably held in check some of the leaders. Leaders who do not have such usable material in their dossiers have been approached to take government posts, mostly as ambassadors and primarily in African countries. The promise of these positions also has materially contributed to a temporary slow-down of Minority activities. However, we do not expect these slow-downs to be of long duration, because there are always new and dissident elements joining these organizations, with the potential power to replace the old leaders. All organizations and their leaders are under constant, 24-hour surveillance. The organizations are:

1 - **The Black Muslims;**
2 - **Student Nonviolent Coordinating Committee (SNCC)**
3 - **Congress of Racial Equality**
4 - **Uhuru Movement;**
5 - **Group On Advanced Leadership (GOAL)**
6 - **Freedom Now Party (FNP)**
7 - **United Black Nationalists of America (UBNA)**
8 - The New Pan-African Movement (TNPAM)
9 - Southern Christian Leadership Conference (SCLC)
10 - The National Urban League (NUL)
11 - The National Association for the Advancement of Colored People (NAACP)
12 - Committee on Racial and Religious Progress **(CORARP)**

NOTE: At the appropriate time, to be designated by the President, the leaders of some of these organizations are to be detained ONLY WHEN IT IS CLEAR THAT THEY CANNOT PREVENT THE EMERGENCY, working with local public officials during the first critical hours. All other leaders are to be detained at once. Compiled lists of Minority leaders have been readied at the National Data Computer Center. It is necessary to use the Minority leaders designated by the President in much the same manner in which we use Minority members who are agents with Central and Federal, and we cannot, until there is no alternative, reveal King Alfred in all its aspects. Minority members of Congress will be unseated at once. This move is not without precedent in American history.

This is an excerpt from a military document that shows and proves why black negro coloured Africans etc make no progress due to infiltration. Noble Drew Ai is one of the supreme examples of the highest level of infiltration, espionage, agent provocateurs and sellouts of Asiatic liberation in the Americas. It is so deep of a sellout that mention could not even be given to the Moorish Science Temple of America in King Alfred Plan. Why would they not give honourable mention in King Alfred Plan to the MSTA? Why wouldn't King Alfred Plan not mention the MSTA if it was infiltrated during the mid to late 1900's and some Moorish elders say as early as 1913? Or did they make mention in MOORS CODE?

Attorney General Preliminary Memo: Department of Defense

This memo is being submitted in lieu of a full report from the Joint Chiefs of Staff. That report is now in preparation. There will be many cities where the Minority will be able to put into the street a superior number of people with a desperate and dangerous will. He will be a formidable enemy, for he is **bound to the Continent by heritage and knows that political asylum will not be available to him in any other counties.**

"One of Ali's opponents was David Ford, the new member he commissioned in the Spring of 1929 to oversee the MSTA while Ali was on trial for the murder of a disenchanted official. Prior to Ali's death (or as Moors claim, the time "he left the physical form"), he renamed his newest disciple Ford-El and released the Chicago temple to him. In November, Ford-El moved to Detroit, where he assumed the names Wallace D. Fard and Wallace D. Fard Muhammad. Later he would organize the Nation of Islam. [25] Upon Ali's death at his South Side home in July of 1929, the unsettled leadership question again split the movement. Of the five disciples battling for the MSTA helm, two factions assumed center stage-- both maintaining headquarters in Chicago and operating under the MSTA banner. The two competing leaders -- E. Mealy-El, Governor and Supreme Grand Sheik of Temple #1, and C. Kirkman-Bey, Supreme Grand Advisor of Temple #9 -- claimed their temples as the national headquarters of the organization. Initially, some temple leaders attended the annual conventions of both groups. Other splits resulted in the reorganization of independent temples, some whose self-proclaimed leaders claimed to be reincarnations of Ali."
- *http://www.freepatentsonline.com/article/Cross Currents/74992665.html*

"The interviews that Essien– Udom carried out with NOI converts, Elijah Muhammad and the groups ministerial body enabled him to gain insight into eclectic religious philosophy of the group, something that had long eluded outsiders. The eclectic amalgam of black nationalism and pseudo Islam that the NOI taught convinced the Nigerian Scholar that the NOI's founder had married the Black nationalism tradition of Marcus Garvey's UNIA with the quasi-Islamic teachings of the MSTA in order to manufacture his OWN separatist ideologies… Essien-Udom's belief that the NOI grew out of the MSTA is well founded… the latter part of Fard's FBI file does contain a few references to his activities in the MSTA"
-*A History of the Nation of Islam By Dawn-Marie Gibson*

It becomes very obvious very early in the studies of the FBI papers that many people who are heads of these 12 infiltrated organizations had some direct or indirect connection to Noble Drew Ali and the Moorish Divine and National Movement that he founded in 1913 but exercised it as the Old Canaanite Temple in Newark, New Jersey.

Ford-El claimed Drew Ali left him in charge and declared himself the founder's <u>reincarnation</u>. Arguments erupted over the issue of successor. Those who had been loyal to Claude Greene Bey argued that Ford-El had not been with the MSTA long enough to succeed Drew Ali, and insisted that Charles Kirkman Bey, one of Greene's closest allies, had the authority to assume the mantle of leadership.

After Noble Drew Ali was assassinated by his own people around him wearing turbans and fezzes, there began infighting for his seat of power, his fame and nobility. Moors were coming out of the woodworks proclaiming themselves the reincarnation of Noble Drew Ali. And because many of the members didn't study what the Prophet presented to the Moors, it was only a matter of time before numbers dwindled. **Edward Mealy El** The first Supreme Grand Sheik of the M.S.T. of A. Appointed to said office by the Holy Prophet himself and was never removed by the Holy Prophet. The only one whom the Holy Prophet trusted to carry out that post. Many Moors that we infiltrators of the Moorish movement were upset that E. Mealy El was made successor by the Prophet.

Many Moors thought E. Mealy El was unqualified. To the Prophet, E. Mealy El demonstrated true faith in the Prophet and this is why, this humble, quiet man was commanded by the Prophet to be the ONLY true successor and head of the Moorish Movement, next to the beneficiaries, Moors.

MAY 27th, 1931
Moorish Science Temple of America
NOBLE DREW ALI, Founder
Home Office: 3718 Prairie Ave. --- Tel. Douglas 2725
Send all official Business to the Home Office in 5 Chicago, Ill.
Care of E. MEALY EL, S.G.S.

ISLAM

Many were there when the decision was handed down. Now they claim the Judge has never passed his decision. There is no cause for them to be like that, only they don't want to be governed by the Truth now, since the Prophet passed, and that is the only hope of our security. One great hindrance to my people is, they don't understand the Words of Truth, Peace & Love as set before them by the Great PROPHET. He said so when he was here and told them if they Understood Language, they would be alright.

I am sorry for them, because not knowing, they blame me for all that has happen. Yet when the Prophet was here, He told them, He Brought The divine Plans of the Ages. And they can't be Changed. And the Plans are called the plans of Redemption and was brought only by A REDEEMER. And this REDEEMER, called Me, Ordained Me, Commissioned Me, and then Appointed Me to My Station, And Instructed Me That I was There to stay, At His absence.

And that all wanted that place, but said, I know who I want there. I know who I want to handle <u>My Money</u>. He further said, You are to collect all money, and pay off all bills, He still said. And you will have to do what I Am doing. You will have to go around to all Temples, and report Back to Me. Time and space won't permit me to say all you want to know, or what I would like to tell you. But I say as I have, to give you who don't know, or have not had the chance to know the Prophet, or be With Him as I was, I had and have a reason for everything I did or have done. And can and will prove my Authority, by His HOLY KORAN AND CONSTITUTION, AND HIS GENERAL AND BY-LAWS.

But the idea is this, THE PLANS ARE DIVINE, and we are going through a crisis and conflict, that must be, before we can be redeemed.

I hope I have made my self clear. If I haven't write me. I love all I haven't a pet any place. No special favors for any; considerate with any; under the five great principles: LOVE, TRUTH, PEACE FREEDOM, AND JUSTICE.

I hope to hear from all soon. And if we expect to meet the prince of Peace, in peace and with joy to our souls, we had better begin to think, talk, walk and act different.

He was made in secret, in the public, He was unmade. Get a program of 1929's Convention. If you haven't one, send for one; read, think, and you will (find/figure) out that the programs are printed before the convention convenes.

Now trust in ALLAH through his PROPHET, and live on. follow anyone else and perish. Peace. Love to all; E. Mealy El S.G.S

Noble Drew Ali is a Prophet and he warned the Moors about the infiltration of the temples. But because Moors didn't study, it took over 50 years for Moors to figure out what Noble Drew Ali brought them. He was very clear, and if you read his literature, rather than following the leaders, one can see, recognize and acknowledge the clarity in which Noble Drew Ali spoke.

FOLLOWING OUR LEADERS

The thousands of Moorish Americans will follow their leaders. Regardless of propaganda put forth by those who have designs to hinder them in the work for the advancement of their people. We will not stop to question the requisites, qualifications nor anything else, so long as our leaders who have investigated and passed on the course of action which we feel is enough endorsement for us to act. We have long known that the first attempt to crush the leaders of any movement or organization is to plant dissension among their followers. Such will never will never be the case with the Moorish Americans, for when we have chosen our leaders that within itself tells the world that we are going to follow them. All of the knocks and slams that come from anyone against our leaders will be ignored by us. Where they lead us we will follow.
Noble Drew Ali

MARCH 11, 1929

Brother Crumbey-Bey the Governor and Chief Head of the Temple in Pittsburgh Pa. Brother Childs-Bey Governor and Chief Head of the Temple in Cleveland Ohio.

These two Brothers are in power by the PROPHET to investigate business etc. of Temple number four in Detroit Michigan, because Lomax-Bey has violated all DIVINE LAWS of the PROPHET even before the Prophets face Feb. 15 1929. He claims that the Prophet has no more power and the finance from Detroit would be in his charge. He wouldn't send any to the Prophet. He yelled with a loud voice, "Look at me. I will guide you through." This is lawful and living evidence spoken before fifteen hundred (1500) people and the Prophet was also present.

I, THE PROPHET, declare his office vacant and the name of Grand Governor discharged. He can only be a member according to LAW because the Moorish Science Temple of America is a DIVINE ORGANIZATION. Each Temple is under Supreme Guidance of the Prophet.

When man fails after being placed Head of the Temple by the Prophet of obeying our Divine laws and constitutions, he is a traitor and enemy of the Divine Creed and unloyal to the National Government U.S.A. to which the movement is to make men and women better citizens.

FROM THE PROPHET,
NOBLE DREW ALI.

E. Mealy El carried out his instruction to the best of his ability knowing the juggernaut called the sellout he was up against.

TO THE HEADS OF ALL TEMPLES

Islam,

These are critical moments, and all Moslems are required to follow instructions.

During the life of our Prophet, he told us many things, but there was many things that he said he couldn't tell, but we would know after while.

Since he passed he left his son who will guide you, now of course the Prophet's laws are alright but there are plenty he couldn't write or put in book form, so someone had to tell you, now some are going to believe it and some are not, but now let me say to you as a brother we loves Israel, please don't be the hardhead.

In the Adept last night we were told not to eat meat, but to eat anything in the fish line with scales on it, that leaves out cat and eel, eat fish and vegetables, etc. but no meat of any kind or any strong drinks until further notice.

please don't do any of these things until you hear from the Grand Body.

PEACE,

Your Brother in Islam

E. MEALY EL. S.G.S.

TEMPLE NO. 11, 817 SOUTH BROAD STREET

Bro. A. H. Payne-El, S.B.M.

3757 South State Street,

Chicago, Illinois

Dear Brother Payne-El,

In reading your letter to Brother Thompson-El a few minutes ago, and in view of the wishes of our PROPHET, as laid down in his laws to me, by himself, I wish to call to our attention to the fact that it was his will that we hold the coming convention of 1929, beginning September the 15th to the 20th of the same month.

My objection is only that the date which was made by the PROPHET be considered as law with me, and remembering also that he said; "as long as you do what I tell you, you will be alright, but when you fail to obey my orders, you will have trouble." Having talked the matter over with all the Governors, I find them all in favor of supporting the date of the Convention as laid down by our PROPHET.

Now, as Business Manager, I am asking you to give away to the time of the PROPHETS choice and arrange your dates accordingly, which begins September 15th to September 20th inclusive, this will also give them more time for preparation for the same.

We must do all we can for Peace, that a progressive advance may manifest itself in all of our actions. This done, all also is well, trusting this meets your approval, I am

Your Brother in Islam,

E. MEALY EL S.G.S.

FORESTERS HALL, 44th AND STATE STREET

ISLAM,

Bro. C. Kirkman Bey, this is to notify you, that the above named Organization, MOORISH SCIENCE TEMPLE OF AMERICA, in Convention, SEPT. 15th to 20th, rescinded by voting out the mistake made by the second annual Convention, of 1929.

And in so doing, you hold your Membership Roll, as when our Prophet was here, and we hope you will still cooperate with the organization under the five principles.

We hope further, that you will comply with this notice, and govern yourself accordingly.

As there is but ONE Supreme Grand Adviser, in the MOORISH SCIENCE TEMPLE OF AMERICA, that being NOBLE DREW ALI, and any one else attempting to be, from now on, is assuming authority of himself, and is liable to the penalties of the LAW.

PEACE.

MOORISH SCIENCE TEMPLE OF AMERICA NOBLE DREW ALI, FOUNDER.

E. MEALY EL, Chairman.

Noble Drew Ali knew what he was doing by putting someone faithful in charge. He knew, in E. Mealy El's heart, that he was for the Nation, not arrogant like many of the other Moors in the Temple using the new found knowledge of self of Moorish Science for selfish gain, while, not recognizing the Holy Prophet. This is the same deceit and same manner described by all the 16 crucified Saints and how the disciples were the problem due to their lack of faith. Noble Drew Ali knew about the sellout and his Moors trying to assassinate him, so he addressed it after he got arrested for trumped up charges for the murder of Claude Green Bey. It is said that Claude Green Bey, splintered off, declaring himself Grand Sheik, taking a number of members of the original temple, but was later stabbed by unknown parties. Drew Ali was arrested for the murder of Claude Green Bey, but never indicted or charges. While detained, Drew Ali wrote 2 letters to address the matter at hand and to teach the Moors about the traitors in the movement. One of the letters are as follows:

TO BE PROCLAIMED AT EVERY MEETING

ISLAM:

I am glad to know that I have a few faithful Moors among you all, and I desire for them to know the Truth, and the Divine Truth. There is a host of Jealousy, about Me, and the Movement now by the same people of our side of the Nation that claim that I was only a joke and unreal; But now since they have found out from the Government Officials and the Nations of the Earth, that this is the only Soul Foundation, that all Asiatics must depend upon, for their Earthly Salvation as American Citizens, They are working every scheme that they can, to disqualify Me, so they may take charge of the situation.

I have notified all these things to you, long ago in the past. It is through the faithful Moors, that attribute to the Movement and Uplifting Funds; The ones that paid their Divine respect to Me and the Movement; will be remembered. That is why I am calling Upon all faithful Moors, to increase their faithfulness to Me Your Prophet, and Your Divine Moorish Movement.

I need finance, and I need it badly. Never before have I needed Finance so badly, as I do at present, so I can shove aside the Discord, that is facing the Nation. It all comes through Jealousy, Because of My Fame and Nobility. The Nations of the World will not recognize the movement, without I, The PROPHET, being Head. It has been proven by My works, which I have performed in the past few Years. -

PROPHET NOBLE DREW ALI

The Great Sellout took place from the inception of the Moorish Divine and National Movement of North America. Being that he was a Prophet, he was well aware of what was going to happen by 1929 to himself, so to protect the Moorish Movement as a standard, from the beginnings of the Movement, he put out critical pieces of information to let the eyes wide open, seeing and knowing new Moors, who he proclaimed will come, use what he presented to put the pieces of the shattered mirror of the Moorish Divine and National Movement together and KNOW THEM SELF when they look in the mirror. The reason unconscious Moors look at the Moorish Divine and National Movement of North America as confusion is because they are looking at a shattered mirror. Not only that, because of the Great Sellout OUTSIDE of the Temples by "black religious leaders" the unconscious Moors labeled negro, black, coloured and Ethiopian/African had no idea about their Moorish Nationality, Birthrights and History. Noble Drew Ali made many powerful statements about the status of the Moorish Movement in comparison to other organizations for the liberation of the Asiatics of North America. In a writing called The Moorish Science Temple of America, Noble Drew Ali made clear his hopes for the Moorish Divine and National Movement.

THE MOORISH SCIENCE TEMPLE OF AMERICA

The Moorish Science Temple of America was founded by the Prophet Noble Drew Ali. Aside from the fact that it is a legally organized religious corporation, It is building on human needs. To this desirable end, in time legitimate means will be found to dispense charity and provide for the mutual assistance of its members in times of distress; to aid in the improvement of health and to encourage the ownership of better homes; to find employment for our members; to teach those fundamental principles which are desired for our civilization such as obedience to law, respect and loyalty to government, tolerance and unity.

It is most earnestly hoped that the Moorish Science Temple of America, will not in any way be confused with any "Back to Africa Movement." Such is not important insofar as American citizens of our group colonizing Africa are concerned.

We, of the Moorish Science Temple of America, like countless other American citizens, know that we must live together here in America in harmony, friendship and goodwill, whatever our race and creed may be.

It is only from a purely religious standpoint (it seems at this time) that we differ from a large number of our fellow Americans. We believe in, and foster the Moslem religion. We believe in the principles of its teachings insofar they can be adopted to American life. We feel that the Christian religion is alright for those who prefer it. In America, religious freedom is guaranteed all under the constitution.

We are Interested in freeing ourselves and our children, from the greatest plight- economic slavery. We believe this can be best done by encouraging, patronizing and establishing our own business enterprises and cultivating our own acres of land. We welcome into our folds men and women of our group of all sections, all trades, occupations and professions of sound mind and good character.

We are friends and servants of humanity. We are dedicated to the purpose of elevating the moral, social, and economic status of our people. We have set about to do this through a wide and comprehensive program embodying the principles of love, truth, peace, freedom, and justice. N.D.A.

Noble Drew Ali SPECIFICALLY SAID TO THE WORLD, It is most earnestly hoped that the Moorish Science Temple of America, will not in any way be confused with any "Back to Africa Movement." What is the Back to Africa Movement that Noble Drew Ali EARNESTLY HOPED the Moorish Science Temple of America would not be confused with? It was the Dirty Moors, who usurped Noble Drew Ali's Fame and Nobility, and under the GUISE of NEGRO, BLACK, COLORED, AFRICAN AND ETHIOPIAN ORGANIZATIONS, CREATED an ASSUMED, COLORABLE JURISDICTION.

Color- An appearance, semblance, or simulacrum, as distinguished from that which Is real. A prima facie or apparent right. Hence, a deceptive appearance; a plausible, assumed exterior, concealing a lack of reality ; a disguise or pretext.

The COLOR OF JURISDICTION CREATED by the "black, negro, coloured, Ethiopian/African leaders" is why Noble Drew Ali wanted no connection to those "back to Africa Movements. We are Moors, indigenous to the Americas and adjoining Atlantis Islands.

When we research black history, it starts at the fall of the Moors in Spain. The so called slaves brought to the Americas by Cristobal Colon were prisoners of war from the Spanish dungeons of the Spanish Inquisition.

Lets backtrack a few centuries.....In the early fifth century A.D., Spain was invaded by Vandals and other Germanic tribes. In the second half of the century, the Visigoths achieved dominance, pushing the Vandals into Africa. The Visigoth kingdom collapsed in 711 when the Moors — North African Muslims — invaded from Morocco. Within a few years the Moors conquered nearly all of the peninsula and advanced into southern France, until turned back by Charles Martel in the Battle of Tours in 732. During this same exact time, in the Americas, there have been civilizations around just as long as those " founding civilizations of the East."

- 711 Mayan Tonina captured Palenque king Kan Xul II.
- 738 Quirigua ruler Cauac Sky sacrificed 18 Rabbit. Mayans
- 750 Teotihuacan was smashed and burned. Mayans
- 761 Mayan Tamarindito sacrificed 4th Petexbatun king.
- 800-1400 Mound builders had cities in Mississippi Valley. Northern America
- 808 Last date was recorded in Mayan Yaxchilan.
- 810 Last date was recorded in Mayan Quirigua.
- 822 Last date was recorded in Mayan Copan.
- 849-1221 Itza Maya occupied Chichen Itza.
- 889 Last date was recorded in Mayan Tikal.
- 900 Zapotec centralized government ended. Mayans
- c. 950 Toltecs became prominent in valley of Mexico.
- 1004-07 Thorvald Erikson explored northeastern America.
- 1030-63 Eight-Deer ruled the Mixtecs. Toltecs
- 1168 Toltec Tollan was destroyed.
- 1200 Pueblo people lived in Mesa Verde. Anasazi
- 1325 Tenochtitlan was founded in Mexico. Aztecs
- 1358 Tlatelolco was founded in Mexico. Aztecs
- 1371-1426 Tezozomoc ruled Tepanecs. Aztecs
- 1372-91 Acamapichtli ruled the Mexica. Aztecs
- 1391-1414 Huitzilihuitl ruled the Mexica. Aztecs
- 1395 Mexica and Tepanecs conquered Tlaxcala. Aztecs
- 1400 Hopi lived peacefully north of Mexico. Anasazi
- 1409-18 Ixtlilxochitl ruled Texcoco. Aztecs

The biggest fraud or color of History in the Americas is who are the true indigenous people? There have always been dark skinned people, or Moors on the land of the Americas, millions of years before Christopher Columbus or Norsemen Visigoths.

" The people who built the great pyramids all over South America, Peru,

Canada, Alaska, and Georgia that scattered all throughout North America along the Mississippi River and it's tributaries are found mounds built out of tons and tons of earth. The people who built them were called the Mound Builders and they were the descendants of the Malian Moor Olmecs. These Moors eventually migrated to North America from Mexico and became known as Washitaw, Yamasee and the Ben-Isma-EL tribe. The Ben-Isma-EL tribe was a collection of what is now known as Lenape, Wapanoag and Nanticoke Indians who migrated to Indiana and Illinois and referred to themselves as "Moors" even though the United States Government continued to classify them as "Negroes" in order to strip them of their Indigenous rights." -*http://pointingbird.tripod.com/lostfeatherintl/id64.htm*

There is enough documented evidence of not all dark skin people coming to America on a slave ship, and until Noble Drew Ali came, that position of indigenous people of America, was held by so called native Indians. When we do what Noble Drew Ali ordered, which was to study, study, study, we will CLEARLY see, without a doubt, that there is no need to go "Back to Africa." And that anyone teaching the concept of "Back to Africa" has abandoned their Moorish birthright and have no connection to the Moorish Divine and National

Movement or their salvation. Back to Africa is color of history. A semblance of History. Fraud. Fraud has no statute of Limitation which means *fraud* does *not* end until the *fraud has* been discovered. Noble Drew Ali discovered the fraud and addressed it Nationally and INTER-Nationally in the Moorish Guide Newspaper in the article Moorish Science Temple of America. Also remember the names of the organizations that were infiltrated and mentioned in King Alfred Plan more so than any other Organization push a Back to Africa perspective. Remember, Noble Drew Ali was assassinated in 1929 by the hands of traitorous Dirty nigger Moors.

The Plenipotentiaries of Prophet Noble Drew Ali

PLENIPOTENTIARY

Noun
 a person, especially a diplomat agent, invested with full power and authority to transact business on behalf of another

As an adjective, *plenipotentiary* refers to that which confers "full powers."

Before the era of rapid international transport or communication (such as radio or telephone), diplomatic mission chiefs were granted full (*plenipotentiary*) powers to represent their government in negotiations with their host nation. Conventionally, any representations made or agreements reached with a plenipotentiary would be recognized and complied with by their government. Historically, the common generic term for high diplomats of the crown or state was *minister*. It therefore became customary to style the chiefs of full ranking missions as **Minister Plenipotentiary**.

Treaty of Peace and Friendship, with additional article; also Ship-Signals Agreement. The treaty was sealed at Morocco with the seal of the Emperor of Morocco June 23, 1786 (25 Shaban, A. H. 1200), and delivered to Thomas Barclay, American Agent, June 28, 1786 (1 Ramadan, A. H. 1200). Original in Arabic. The additional article was signed and sealed at Morocco on behalf of Morocco July 15, 1786 (18 Ramadan, A. H. 1200). Original in Arabic. The Ship-Signals Agreement was signed at Morocco July 6, 1786 (9 Ramadan, A. H. 1200). Original in English.

Certified English translations of the treaty and of the <u>additional article</u> were incorporated in a document signed and sealed by the **Ministers Plenipotentiary** of the United States, Thomas Jefferson at Paris January 1, 1787, and John Adams at London January 25, 1787.

There were 5 Moors who were Adepts, or disciples of Noble Drew Ali and 4 of theme became millionaires because they went against the Prophet and made a connection to the Moorish Movement and Back to Africa Movements. The power, that appears to be behind back to Africa and Pan African Nationalism is Moorish Nationality.

Prophet F. S. Cherry established the Church of God, the Pillar Ground of Truth for All Nations, a Jewish movement in Philadelphia retaining numerous Christian elements. Although Cherry was a charismatic orator who was fluent and literate in Hebrew and Yiddish, little is known or recorded about his humble beginnings. His personal accounts depict a completely self-educated seaman and laborer who traveled the world until "the Lord touched him and appointed him a prophet," thus leading Cherry back to America to teach African <u>Americans</u> that "the true Jews are black and that Jesus was black." As a religious figure attracting southern migrants, Cherry used the Talmud and the Old Testament to bolster his belief that Jews of the European Diaspora were impostors, and his followers were the true Israelites. While the Church of God existed other organizations made the claim of being the "Black Jews" including William S. Crowdy, The Church of God and Saints of Christ, and after Crowdy's death in 1908, the church continued to grow under the leadership of William Henry Plummer, who moved the organization's headquarters to its permanent location in <u>Belleville</u>, <u>Virginia</u>, in 1921. In 1936, the Church of God and Saints of Christ had more than 200 tabernacles" (congregations) and 37,000 members. The distinguished Elder Rabbi Wentworth A. Mathew led the Commandment Keepers of the Living God also known as the Royal Order of Ethiopian Hebrews but kept to the protocol laid down by Noble Drew Ali and attached the pedigree Moorish to his Hebrew Organization. Ask the Hebrew Israelites today, why are they fronting? Why are they denying the people their birthright?

Arnold Josiah Ford's contributions to the UNIA, however, were not limited to musical and religious matters.

He and E.L. Gaines <u>wrote</u> the handbook of rules and regulation for the paramilitary African Legion (which was modeled after the Zionist Jewish Legion) and developed guidelines for the Black Cross Nurses. He served on committees, spoke at rallies, and was elected one of the delegates representing the 35,000 members of the New York chapter at the First International Convention of Negro Peoples of the World, held in 1920 at Madison Square Garden. There the governing body adopted the red, black, and green flag as its ensign, and Ford's song "Ethiopia" became the "Universal Ethiopian Anthem," which the UNIA constitution required be sung at every gathering. During that same year, Ford published the *Universal Ethiopian Hymnal*. Ford was a proponent of replacing the term "Negro" with the term "Ethiopian," as a general reference to people of African descent. Following Garvey's arrest in 1923, the UNIA loss much of its internal cohesion. Since Ford and his small band of followers were motivated by principals that were independent of Garvey's charismatic appeal, they were repeatedly approached by government agents and asked to testify against Garvey at trial, which they refused to do. However, in 1925, Ford brought separate law suits against Garvey and the UNIA for failing to pay him royalties from the sale of recordings and sheet music, and in 1926 the judge ruled in Ford's favor. Several black religious leaders were experimenting with Judaism in various degrees between the two world wars. Ford then worked with Mordecai Herman and the Moorish Zionist Temple, until, it is said, they had an altercation over theological and financial issues. It seems mis-concepts and fiat always comes between freedom for people and their leaders.

Bishop Charles Manuel "Sweet Daddy" Grace was born <u>Marcelino Manuel da Graca</u>, January 25, 1884, in Brava Cape Verde Islands, a Portuguese possession off the west coast of Africa. He came to America on a ship called Freedom in 1903 and settled in New Bedford, Massachusetts. After leaving his <u>job</u> as a railway cook, Grace began using the title "Bishop." In 1919, Daddy Grace, as parishioners knew him, built the first House of Prayer in West Wareham, Massachusetts at the cost of thirty-nine dollars. He later established branches in <u>Charlotte</u>, <u>North Carolina</u> and **<u>Newark, New Jersey</u>** . Throughout the 1920s and 1930s, Daddy Grace traveled America preaching and establishing the United House of Prayer for all People. The **constitution and bylaws of The United House of Prayer**, promulgated in 1929, stated that the purpose of the organization in pertinent part was "to erect and maintain places of worship and assembly where all people may gather prayer and to worship the Almighty God, irrespective of denomination or creed." He traveled extensively throughout the segregated South in the 1920s and 1930s preaching to integrated congregations years before the civil rights struggles of the 1950s and 1960s and the religious ecumenical movements which followed. One of the many criticisms made against Grace is the following statement which Grace is to have allegedly made in the early 1940s: "Salvation is by Grace only. Grace has given God a vacation, and since He is on vacation, don't worry about Him. If you sin against God, Grace can save you, but if you sin against Grace, God cannot save you." Many Christian leaders were members of the Moorish Science Temple of America, or had direct beef with him because he was exposing the fraud of the 14th and 15th Amendment that the "black Christian preachers" were using to keep the people part of their pseudo religious institutions. The Ku Klux Klan are the grand protectors of the Christian creed and black Christian leaders who are free masons know this and STILL promote and endorse their people being Christians knowing the Klan is lynching niggers for wanting to be Christian. Through census records, ship manifests, and FBI files, this dissertation documents the varied official racial classifications of Grace, a man who regarded himself as white and Portuguese, but who most Americans believed to be black. One common theme that those grassroots religious organizations expressed was the need for a deliverer. When u research these black leaders on your own you will see that most of them founded organizations under the title of the Prophet, or messenger which Noble Drew Ali is that one sent by Allah with fame and nobility to redeem the Asiatics of America.

Father Divine (George Baker) was a finesse master and was sharp enough to capitalize on the economic crisis and the spiritual void of illiterate, economically deprived so called black, negro and coloured southern migrants. Baker began his career in 1899 as an assistant to Father Jehovia (Samuel Morris), the founder of an independent religious group. During his early adult years, Baker was influenced by Christian Science and New Thought. Father Divine self proclaimed himself one specifically guided by God. He preached Christianity and mysticism; and being that he was taught by Noble Drew Ali, he was so adept that his congregation believed him to be God in person. He was clever enough to know that when you feed a person when he or she is starving you have indeed won his or her loyalty. Thus during the Depression, which was caused by Noble Drew Ali going to the Pan American Conference in Cuba in 1928, Father Divine provided his followers with employment through his Sayville Employment Center, and he provided them food, shelter and weekly prayer services. To the condemned, disdained, overlooked so called negro black and coloured, their prayers had been answered, and as a result his followers worshipped him as God. He subsequently changed his name to Father God Major Jealous Divine, Dean of the Universe. He called his followers "Angels", just like Noble Drew Ali taught the Moors the Asiatics were Angels and they, father Divines followers, were required to adhere to strict discipline. He promised his true followers eternal life, for he considered death the final weakness. His sacred text was titled "The New Day." He went on to state that everyone could be a part of the American society, which sounds very similar to Noble Drew Ali's teachings. However, he claimed that this could only be actualized in a government under God, and Father Divine was God. Father Divine was an agent and a sign of an agent provocateur are contradiction in the teachings. For example, the movement builds on the principles of Americanism, brotherhood, Christianity, democracy, and Judaism, with the understanding that all "true" religions teach the same basic truths. The fact he taught democracy shows the hypocrisy since Drew Ali taught his plenipotentiaries enforce the Constitution of the United States of America, which doesn't even mention the word democracy. On the one hand, he was very attracted to pale European America, and he even married European American women; on the other hand, he accentuated and actualized Mr. Garvey's position which stated Black people were superior and whites were inferior, but didn't teach that the people were not negro black coloured, which is another CLEAR sign to the wise about who was involved in the great sellout. Divine declared that he was Negro and God dwelled in him; to his followers and other Negroes/Black people, he declared that they were also Negroes and they were like unto him.

"Heavens were opened across North America as well as in Europe, and, although most of its adherents were African Americans, the movement also attracted many whites (approximately one-fourth of its membership). The Heavens and related businesses brought in millions of dollars in revenue for the Peace Mission. Their success, however, also brought accusations of racketeering against Father Divine that, like the allegations of child abuse that were made against the movement, proved to be unfounded. In 1942 Father Divine moved to suburban Philadelphia, in part to avoid paying a financial judgment in a suit brought by a former movement member. Four years later he married Edna Rose Ritchings, a European Canadian member who, as Mother Divine, succeeded her husband as the movement's leader in 1965. Some contemporary critics also claimed he was a charlatan, and some suppose him to be one of the first modern cult leaders to "black Americans" coming out of slavery.

Sweet Daddy Grace.
Notice the occult fingernails.

Father God Major Jealous Divine

Among those associated with the Moorish Science Temple was a peddler named Wallace D. Fard (or Wali Fard Muhammad) and the son of sharecroppers and former slaves **Elijah Poole**. In 1930, claiming that he was Noble Drew Ali reincarnated, Fard El founded the Nation of Islam in Detroit, Michigan, and designated his able assistant, Elijah Muhammad, originally Elijah Poole Bey, to establish the Nation' second centre in Chicago. When problems erupted in the Detroit headquarters in 1934, Elijah Muhammad stepped in and took control. While Fard retired into obscurity, Elijah taught that Fard was THE Prophet (in the Muslim sense) and a Saviour (in the Christian sense) and the very presence of Allah in Man, matter of fact said Fard Muhammad was Allah.

"WE BELIEVE that *Allah* (God) appeared in the Person of Master W. *Fard* Muhammad, July, 1930" - Nation of Islam website

"The Moors of North Africa had a splendid and glorious history, where Tarik Ibn Zaid in the 8th Century took civilization to Europe who were experiencing the Dark Ages. Some argue that W.F. Muhammad and Elijah Muhammad borrowed a lot of its teachings and theology from Ali and the Moorish Science Temple. " -John G. Jackson and Willis N. Huggins; "A Guide to Studies in African History

Poole fled Georgia for Detroit in 1923 in the freedom from slavery pattern of "black migration" to the north. In Detroit, he worked in several industrial plants and joined a variety of organizations-most noted, Marcus Garvey's proto-black-nationalist movement, the United Negro Improvement Association (UNIA), and the Black Shiners; After an arrest for drunkenness in 1926, Poole also joined the Moorish Science Temple of America (MSTA) and converted to ISLAMISM, becoming intensely involved in the institution and in spreading of the MSTA doctrine.

The MSTA organization had nothing in common with the standard version of Islam coming from the East, but it was the first to forge a 20th-century link between that religion and subjugated Moors in America. In the ensuing struggle for power after Noble Drew Ali was assassinated, three major factions emerged, all based in Chicago. One was led by a very recent convert to the MSTA named David Ford El, who quickly moved to Detroit and renamed both himself (Wallace D. Fard) and his faction - the Allah Temple of Islam (ATI). It must be understood to the reader, that ANY organization for the liberation of Melanin beings, that teaches the members must change/correct their name, got that idea from Noble Drew Ali. The rules of the MSTA is that all members must proclaim their nationality and in making that proclamation, the member corrects their slave name by attaching El or Bey to it or correcting the name completely to a Moorish title.

This new sect founded by David Ford El retained many of the MSTA's customs and ideas, but it also introduced new elements of propaganda to confuse most of the illiterate masses in 1930, including the theme that there is such a thing as "whites" and that they are devils and as well had a paramilitary unit called the Fruit of Islam. The Fruit of Islam has its foundation in the MSTA Moorish Unified Front Toward Islam or M.U.F.T.I. It is said that in early 1931, Elijah Poole met Fard and quickly became his enthusiastic disciple, receiving in return the "original" name of Elijah Karriem. A year later, Fard further rewarded Elijah by making him Supreme Master of the ATI and changing his name yet again, now to Elijah Muhammad. Over the course of their partnership, Fard and Elijah Muhammad also elevated Fard's own theological status - from Allah's Messiah to Allah himself - with Muhammad taking over the role of Messenger.

Noble Drew Ali who traveled extensively in the East and in Africa, that he called Amexem, concluded that so called "blacks were not Ethiopians" as proclaimed by his contemporaries, but that they were Asiactics. Keep in mind AGAIN the contractions. Farad and Elijah used the term Asiatic Black man, when Drew Ali, their leader specifically taught that we are Moors, descendants of Moroccans born in America. He taught that the European inquisitionist Nations stripped Moors of their nationality and placed them in the role of a slave. Making a deal with Fard, the authorities let him out of a psychiatric ward on condition he shut down the ATI; Fard agreed, but then tricked the police by changing the ATI's name to Nation of Islam (NoI) and keeping it alive. He was finally forced to leave Detroit in mid-1934. Its no different that groups called Aboriginal Law Firms that change the name to a Society. Why?????

Muhammad hated the United States, not the United States of America as he was taught by Noble Drew Ali and loved its enemies, especially non-Caucasian ones. And so he rejoiced in the Japanese victory at Pearl Harbor in 1941, not only refusing to register for military service but instructing his followers to do likewise. Arrested for draft evasion in May 1942 and getting out in August 1946. If he stuck to the principles the Prophet laid down he wouldn't have been arrested for draft evasion. The Nation had been kept alive during those years by his wife Clara and other faithful acolytes. It was at this point that Malcolm X appears and instills a resurrection for Elijah Muhammad.

" **After the establishment of Clock of Destiny National Cultural Club,** C. M. Bey moved forward to <u>form</u> another group. At one time there were as many as four (4) different organizations headed under the Clock of Destiny National Cultural Club operating in the city of Cleveland. Even though C.M. Bey was closely affiliated with James Johnson Bey in 1956, and considered him as a vital functioning entity for the distribution of this knowledge, James Johnson Bey formed the now existing Moorish-American Institute in 1970, which was housed at 2844 Woodhill Road, Cleveland, Ohio. **The Institute has always maintained original teachings of Noble Drew Ali** passed down through the various teachers since 1965 and prior to the establishment of the Moorish Science Temple and its acquisition to religious connotations. As direly expressed, so as not to cause confusion to those who are seeking religious principals, Moorish-American institute is not a religious organization or church. Our sole structure is based upon logic of universal knowledge and scientific definitions thereof. **Moorish-American Institute** specializes in the teaching of Moorish history. Zodiac Science, yoga, and many other sciences that tend to aid humanity in understanding the universe which surrounds, and, is within us. When the true Moorish history is known to the Asiatics, they will no longer have a reason to resent the Europeans. From that point, commissioned by Noble Drew Ali, he set out to write the necessary documents, books and Cosmo Constitution Law of the Great Seal that the world may be free. C. M. Bey registered his work with the Library of Congress in 1947 coded under the USC Title 22 Chapter 2 Sec. 141 under judicial protection. At this point he began to go from place to place to lecture and working to restore the lost people. Namely those classified as Negroes, Black, African Americans, West Indian etc. but more especially the dark skinned people here in America called Negroes to their constitutional heritage, birthright, and nationality which would free them from their enslaved causes by the use of their animalistic time Negros and slave. He worked faithfully for 10 years from 1947-1957. It was this time he was stricken by a stroke in which speech impairment resulted. After recovery from his stroke C.M. Bey began to teach others to teach: from 1957-1973. He worked diligently and faithfully writing literature so the <u>job</u> of uplifting of fallen humanity may be carried on.

Rvbeypublications.com and *clockofdestiny.com*

Charles Mosley Bey Ph. D., L.L D., 3rd 33rd 360 Degree Master Mason, Free Moorish Master Astrologer, Moorish Constitution Law Giver.

It is alleged that after being released from prison, Noble Drew Ali was beaten by Chicago police, and released on bond pending an indictment. Noble Drew Ali was released into the hands of the treacherous, deceitful, unfaithful dirty Moors and it was them that beat him to a pulp. He died shortly afterwards, in 1929. It was speculated that his death was due to injuries received at the hands of the police, although the exact circumstances of his death are unknown. He was never brought up on charges for any involvement in the death of Claude Green Bey. As well his death certificate was altered to say he died of pneumonia, and there was never an investigation as to who killed Green Bey since the Prophet wasn't charged for the murder.

C.M Bey was the ONLY one of the Adept disciples of the Noble Prophet Drew Ali to do his job among the five Adepts under Noble Drew Ali. When we look at he history of all organizations after the Prophet was assassinated, we recognize who the sellouts are. The sellouts are the ones that kept the slave brands as identities, when they were ALL taught by the Prophet that we are not negro, black, coloured or Ethiopian, we are Moors. The sellout is so great due to the obvious fact, that all these groups for the liberation and redemption of Asiatics in the World, specifically North America and the Atlantis Islands (West Indies), identify the people with slave brands negro, black, coloured, Ethiopian, African etc.., which causes them to be mentally enslaved. All the leaders of these slave tag organizations have made millions of dollars and still continue to make millions of dollars at the expense of their own. The people need to accept the fact that the Only sole foundation for the redemption of Asiatics is through the connection to the Moorish Movement. And to stress the point, it is EARNESTLY hoped that the Moorish Science Temple of America will not be compared to any "back to Africa Movement".

" ... Ali is of interest for a number of reasons; he so-called received an official governmental character from President Woodrow Wilson, recognizing the Moorish Science Temple of America as s sovereign Islamic group and recognized that black Americans had a duly legalized nationality called Moorish Americans. This nationality or racial/ethnic recognition according to Ali afforded blacks certain legal and constitutional rights and even recognition within United Nations based on blacks' linage being tied to the Moors of Africa." - Robert L. Uzzel, "The Moorish Science Temple: A Religion Influenced by Prince Hall Masonry".

Marcus Garvey

"Within modern times the Negro race <u>has not had any real statesmen</u>, and the masses of our people have always accepted the intentions and actions of the statesmen and leaders of other races as being directed in our interest as a group in conjunction with the interests of others. <u>Such a feeling on our part caused us to believe that the Constitution of the United States was written for Negroes, as well as the Constitutions of England, France, Italy, Germany and other countries where Negroes happen to have their present domicile, either as citizens or as subjects.</u>"- Philosophies and Opinions, Chapter 4.

"My enemies in America have done much to hold me up to public contempt and ridicule, but have failed. They believe that the only resort is to stir up <u>national</u> prejudice against me, in that I was not born within the borders of the United States of America. I am not in the least concerned about such a propaganda, because <u>I have traveled the length and breath of America</u> and I have discovered that among the fifteen million of my race, only those who have exploited and lived off the ignorance of the masses are concerned with where I was born. The masses of the people are looking for leadership; they desire sincere, honest guidance in racial affairs. As proof of this I may mention, that <u>the largest number of members in the Universal Negro Improvement Association (of which I am President-General) are to be found in America, and are *native born Americans.*</u> I know these people so well and I love them so well, that I would not for one minute think that they would fall for such an insidious propaganda." – Honourable Messiah Marcus Garvey- DOB Aug 17th 1887

> "Any leadership that teaches to depend on another race is a race that will enslave you. We need a leadership of our own to make us FREEMEN"
>
> "The world is indebted to us for the benefits of civilization. They stole our arts and sciences...so why should we be ashamed of ourselves?"
>
> "THE NEGRO IS CRYING OUT FOR A MOHAMMED, A PROPHET WHO WILL BRING HIM THE KORAN OF ECONOMIC AND INTELLIGENT WELFARE"
>
> -Messiah Marcus Garvey

The Messiah considered what European Americans did to the "Negro" a crime to the "Black" race and called for a united front against the disenfranchisement, lynchings and utter disrespect for the race as a whole.

Messiah Marcus Garvey visited Toronto in 1924 to establish a branch of the Universal Negro Improvement Association (UNIA). Barred from entering the United States, Garvey attempted to implement in Montreal and in Hamilton. During October 1928 he went to visit UNIA branches but was blocked by immigration authorities. In 1937, however, he held a regional UNIA conference in Toronto, was principal of a summer school in African philosophy in Toronto, and visited Nova Scotia and New Brunswick.

At the 1937 meeting he inaugurated his School of African Philosophy, lecturing to selected students after the convention adjourned, and later offering transcripts as a correspondence course through his London office. Filled with Garvey's philosophy of success and prosperity, the series of lessons were designed to prepare UNIA officials and organizers for leadership positions. Garvey assigned the nine graduates of the initial course in 1937 to commissions over specific regions in the United States and Canada.

" The civilization of today has gone <u>drunk and crazy with it's power and by such is seeks through injustices, fraud and lies to crush the unfortunate.</u> But if I am apparently crushed by the system of influence and <u>misdirected power</u>, my cause shall rise again to <u>plague the conscience of the corrupt.</u> For this I am satisfied, and for you, I repeat, I am glad to suffer and even die. Again, I say, cheer up, for better days are ahead. I shall write the history that will inspire millions that are coming and leave the posterity of our enemies to reckon with the hosts for the deeds of their fathers."

Marcus Mosiah Garvey, II

Marcus Garvey: Founded the U.N.I.A, Africa for the Africans, Self Sufficiency, Unity, Black Nationalism, Back to Africa, Declaration of Rights of the Negro Peoples of the World, Established a newspaper. And issued membership cards.

Noble Drew Ali: Founded the Moorish Science Temple of America, Nationality and Birthrights, Love, Truth, Peace, Freedom and Justice, Indigenous to North America, Divine Constitution and By-Laws, established a newspaper and issued NATIONALITY cards.

Marcus Garvey: Mob violence and injustice never helped a race or NATION, and because of this knowledge as gathered from the events of all ages, we as a people in this new age desire to love all mankind not in a social sense, but keeping with the Divine Injunction "MAN LOVE THY BROTHER"- Philosophies and Opinions

Noble Drew Ali: ... And when ye separate in the world, remember the relation that bindeth you to love and unity; and prefer not a stranger before thy own blood. If thy brother is in adversity, assist him. If thy sister in in trouble forsake her not. So shall the fortunes of thy fathers contribution to the support of the whole race; and his care be continued to you all, in your love to each other- Holy Koran of the Moorish Science Temple

Marcus Garvey: *"Where did the name of the organization come from? It was while speaking to a West Indian Negro who was a passenger with me from Southampton, who was returning home to the West Indies from Basutoland with his Basuto wife, that I further learned of the horrors of native life in Africa. He related to me in conversation such horrible and pitiable tales that my heart bled within me. Retiring from the conversation to my cabin, all day and the following night I pondered over the subject matter of that conversation, and at midnight, lying flat on my back, the vision and thought came to me that I should name the organization the Universal Negro Improvement Association and African Communities (Imperial) League. Such a name I thought would embrace the purpose of all black humanity. Thus to the a name was born, a movement created, and a man became known."*

Noble Drew Ali: "Sharif [Noble] Abdul Ali; in America he would be known as Noble Drew Ali. On his return to the United States in 1913 he had a dream in which he was ordered to found a movement "to uplift fallen humanity by returning the nationality, divine creed and culture to persons of Moorish descent in the returning the nationality, divine creed and culture to persons of Moorish descent in the Western Hemisphere teaching the esoteric wisdom derived from the secret circle of Eastern Sages, the Master Adepts of Moorish Science."- Moorsgate.com

Marcus Garvey: "Point me to a weak nation and I will show you a people oppressed, abused, taken advantage of by others. Show me a weak race and I will show you a people reduced to serfdom, peonage and slavery. Show me a well organized nation, and I will show you a people and a nation respected."

Noble Drew Ali: Come good people, because I, the Prophet am sent to redeem this nation from mental slavery which you have now, need everyone of you who think that your situation can be better. This is a field open to strong men and women to uplift the nation and take your place in the affairs of men.

Marcus Garvey: "Let us in shaping our destiny set before us the qualities of human JUSTICE, LOVE, CHARITY, MERCY AND EQUITY. Upon suck foundation let us build a race, and I feel that the God who is Divine, The almighty Creator of the world, shall forever bless this race of ours, and who to tell that we shall not teach men the way to life liberty and true human happiness?"

Noble Drew Ali: Then the Lion and the Lamb can lie down together in yonder hills. And Neither will be harmed because LOVE, TRUTH, PEACE, FREEDOM AND JUSTICE will be reigning in the land. In those days the United States will be one of the greatest civilized and prosperous governments of the world, but If the above principles are not carried out by the citizens and my people in this government, the worst is yet to come.

The Fez is represented in Moorish Science as the HEXALPHA. The Hex Alpha is the Star of David, the Seal of Solomon and the symbol of the Moorish Fez. The relation of H.I.M to the Solomonic dynasty isn't literal, it's the SECRET LESSON that H.I.M belonged to the ANCIENT MOORISH EMPIRE, Through Empres Menen, that existed since the time of HATSHEPSUT who is, the QUEEN OF SHEBA, who is Ma'at-ka-Ra (Makare), Makeda in Ethiopian text KEBRA NEGAST and Bilquis in the Quran.

"The grad cap is a fez with square on top. This shows u that this is the base of your education NOT the end. When you remove the square revealing the circle7 you now have a 360 degree education. The tassel represents the suns rays or knowledge." — Aseer the Duke of Tiers

Marcus Garvey Man Know Thy Self: To me man has no master but God. Man in his authority is a SOVEREIGN LORD. As for the individual man, so for the individual race. This feeling makes man so courageous, so bold, as to make it impossible for his brother to intrude upon his rights.

Noble Drew Ali Man Know Thy Self: Know they self and the pride of his creation, the line uniting divinity and matter behold a part of Allah himself within thee; remember thine own dignity; nor dare descend to evil or to meanness. If you are not careful, your own brother will try put you back into slavery.

Marcus Garvey: Government is not infallible. Government in only an executive control, a centralized authority for the purpose of expressing the will of the people. Before you have a government you must have the people. Without the people there can be no government. The government must be, therefore, an expression of the will of the people.

Noble Drew Ali: Money doesn't make the man, it is free national standards and power that make a man and nation. The wealth of all national governments, gold and silver and commerce belong to the citizens alone and without your national citizenship by name and principles you have no true wealth.

NOTE: Arnold Josiah Ford, was a member and figure head in the Moorish Zionist Temple as well as the U.N.I.A and M.S.T.A. He also had strong relationship with Noble Drew Ali as evidenced by Noble Drew Ali quoting him in the Industrious Acts of the Moors:

"The primitive colors alone were used, says Ford, by the Egyptians, Greeks, and Arabs, in the early period of art, and they prevail in the Alhambra wherever the artist has been Arabic or Moorish."

Arnold Josiah Ford

A **flag** is a piece of cloth, often flown from a pole or mast, generally used symbolically for signaling or identification. The term *flag* is also used to refer to the graphic design employed by a flag, or to its depiction in another medium. A **banner** is a flag or other piece of cloth bearing a symbol, logo, slogan or other message. Banner-making is an ancient craft. The word derives from late Latin *bandum*, a cloth out of which a flag is made (Latin *banderia*, Italian *bandiera*). German developed the word to mean an official edict or proclamation and since such written orders often prohibited some form of human activity, *bandum* assumed the meaning of a ban, control, interdict or excommunication. *Banns* has the same origin meaning an official proclamation, and *abandon* means to change loyalty or disobey orders, semantically "to leave the cloth or flag".

Red, Black and Green are the oldest national colors known to man. They are used as the flag of the Black Liberation Movement in America today, but actually go back to the Zinj Empires of ancient Africa, which existed thousands of years before Rome, Greece, France, England or America. The Red, or the blood, stands as the top of all things. We lost our land through blood; and we cannot gain it except through blood. We must redeem our lives through the blood. Without the shedding of blood there can be no redemption of this race. However, the bloodshed and sorrow will not last always. The Red significantly stands in our flag as a reminder of the truth of history, and that men must gain and keep their liberty, even at the risk of bloodshed. The Black is in the middle. The Black man in this hemisphere has yet to obtain land which is represented by the Green. The acquisition of land is the highest and noblest aspiration for the Black man on this continent, since without land there can be no freedom, justice, independence, or equality.

The Flag of Morocco is the present day flag of the foremothers and forefathers of the Moorish. Morocco was the capitol of the old Moorish Empire and has been ruled under various influential cultural names as Carthaginian, Ottoman, Phoenician and Arabian. True Moroccans were the pride of West Africa because of their being custodian of the Ancient Egyptian Mystery System.

#19. What kind of a flag is the Moorish? It is a red flag with a five pointed green star in the center.

#20. What do the five the five points represent? Love, Truth, Peace, Freedom and Justice.

#21. How old is our flag? It is over 50,000 years old.

So in ACTUALITY the TRUE RBG Flag of the Pan African, Black power movement is the Moroccan/ Moorish Flag. A RED flag, with a GREEN Star, outlined in BLACK.

Immediately after the signing of the Emancipation Proclamation in America, the white man started to think how he could solve the new problem of the Negro. He saw that the Negro could not be slaughtered by whole sale killing in that it would be a blot on American civilization, he therefore had to resort to some means of solving the problem, which meant the extinction of the Negro in America.

"The plan is to throw them off and let them starve economically and die off themselves, or emigrate elsewhere, we care not where. Then no one can accuse us of being inhuman to the Negro as we have not massacred him." - Philosophies and Opinions of Marcus Garvey

Dusé Mohamed Ali (Bey Effendi)

Bey is a title for chieftain, traditionally applied to the leaders of small tribal groups. According to some sources, the word "Bey" is of Turkish language In historical accounts, many Turkish, other Turkic and Persian leaders are titled Bey, Beg, Bek, Bay, Baig or Beigh. They are all the same word with the simple meaning of "lord".

Effendi, Effendy or **Efendi** is a title of nobility meaning a lord or master. Duse was well known in the Americas due to his African Times and Orient Review publications. The paper advocated Pan-African and Pan-Asian nationalism and founded in 1912 in London. Covered issues in the United States, the Caribbean, West Afrika, South Africa, and Egypt, as well as in Asia, including India, China, and Japan.

In 1912 Ali launched *African Times and Orient Review*, the first newspaper in England owned and published by a black person. Through this publication, he developed relationships with a number of black intellectuals, including Booker T. Washington, W.E.B. Du Bois, Alain Locke, and Marcus M. Garvey. He became particularly close to Garvey and joined Garvey's United Negro Improvement Association (UNIA) where he serving as the foreign secretary and the head of African Affairs. Ali left the UNIA following Garvey's 1927 deportation from the United States.

Duse Mohamad Ali's book on the History of Egypt was well known among the ELITE African American intellectuals. Marcus Garvey worked on the paper between 1912 and 1913 and was heavily influenced by Ali. When Duse Mohamed Ali came to America he worked for Garvey's United Negro Improvement Association (UNIA), His profound knowledge of African history led to his election to membership in the Negro Society for Historical Research and later to the American Negro Academy. Ali contributed articles on African issues to Garvey's *Negro World*, headed a department on African affairs. The Garveyite hymn and its Islamic wording in the first stanza: Father of all creation Allah Omnipotent Supreme O'er every nation God bless our President Garvey's slogan, Africa for the Africans, at home and abroad was indicative of the pride and dignity he received from Duse Muhammad Ali. Another of Ali's influence on Garvey can be seen in the Garvey motto One God, One Aim, One Destiny, the one God aspect being akin to the Islamic emphasis on the oneness of God or God's unity.

A graduate of Yale University (1895) with a B.A., **William H. Ferris** (left) subsequently took on the role of writer and lecturer. He was a Harvard Divinity School student from 1897-1899, graduating Harvard with an M.A. in Journalism in 1900. After teaching at Tallahassee State College, Florida Baptist College (1900-1901) he worked for a number of newspapers from 1902-1903. He continued teaching during the years 1903-1905 at Henderson Normal School and Kittrell College in North Carolina. Ferris became pastor of Christ Congregational Church from 1904 to 1905. In 1908 he wrote a book entitled "*Typical Negro Traits*". From 1910-12 he was given charge of the "colored" missions of A.M.E. Zion Church of Lowell and Salem, Massachusetts as a lecturer at white churches. He went on to write "*The African Abroad; or his Evolution in Western Civilization: Tracing his development under Caucasian Milieus*" in 1913.

John Edward Bruce (1856–1924), New York-based intellectual, journalist, and Garveyite, was a key figure in linking individuals in Africa, the West Indies, and the United States in pan-African causes. In 1911 in New York, he co-founded with Arthur Schomburg the Negro Society for was well known to many leading Africans, particularly in Historical Research.

John Edward Bruce (L) pictured with a brother Moor.

He was one of the best-known writers and editors to work on the *Negro World.*. Bruce served as American correspondent for the South African *Ilanga lase Natal*. Because of such ties and the wide distribution of his syndicated column, he West Africa. He corresponded with several African intellectuals, politicians, and businesspeople and often hosted African visitors to the United States. His close acquaintances and admirers included Mojola Agbebi, Edward Wilmot Blyden, Dusé Mohamed Ali, John L. Dube, Solomon Plaatje, Joseph Casely Hayford, James E. K. Aggrey, and Moses Da Rocha, as well as American intellectuals Carter Woodson and Arthur Schomburg.

During his long career as a crusading journalist, Bruce moved increasingly toward support for black nationalism at home and abroad. He was at first critical of Garvey but devoted the last six years of his life to passionate support for the UNIA. He became a writer and editor for the *Negro World* and was awarded the UNIA honorary title of Duke of Uganda. Garvey delivered the eulogy at Bruce's 1924 Liberty Hall funeral, which was attended by some five thousand mourners (NN-Sc, JEB; William Glenn Cornell, "The Life and Thought of John Edward Bruce".

James Wormley Jones (right) was an African-American policeman, World War I veteran, and FBI agent. Jones is most widely known for being the first African-American FBI special agent. Jones was appointed as the first African-American special agent on November 19, 1919 by Bureau of Investigation director A. Bruce Bielaski. Jones was assigned to a new section of the Justice Department created to track the activities of groups perceived as subversive. His work there was under the direct supervision of J. Edgar  Hoover. During his time in the FBI, Jones served in New York and Pittsburgh. In New York he was assigned to infiltrate the Universal Negro Improvement Association under the leadership of Marcus Garvey. Although he was seeking evidence of subversive activities during the "Red Scare" of 1919, Jones' work led to the arrest and trial of Garvey on mail fraud charges.

While conducting his surveillance, Jones adopted the code number 800 for his reports. He apparently knew that his clandestine role was not well concealed. During a March 1920 speech at the UNIA Liberty Hall he took special pains to point out to the audience that he was indeed of African ancestry, although he had the appearance of a person of Caucasian or European ancestry. Nevertheless, he engendered the trust of the UNIA leadership to such an extent that he was able to gain responsibility for registering all incoming correspondence. Jones Report of UNIA infiltration: "With Garvey's future uncertain, speculation arose as to who might succeed him. Jones and others within the UNIA thought that Duse Mohamed Ali was a likely candidate- Amy Jacques Garvey feared such a prospect, knowing that her influence would disappear if Ali gained power. Worried that Ali would attract "the better class of negro" and make UNIA "an organization that will have to be reckoned with", Jones sowed the seeds of dissension. Ali invited John Mitchell editor of the RICHMOND PLANET, to address the UNIA members. Mitchell advised them to find a new leader if they were dissatisfied. Jones promised to see that Garvey gets this information about Mitchells speech".

Nigger Addiction Withdrawal
El Hajj Malik El Shabazz

"I realized racism isn't just a black and white problem. It's brought bloodbaths to about every nation on earth at one time or another. Brother, remember the time that white college girl came into the restaurant — the one who wanted to help the Muslims and the whites get together — and I told her there wasn't a ghost of a chance and she went away crying? Well, I've lived to regret that incident. In many parts of the African continent I saw white students helping black people. Something like this kills a lot of argument. I did many things as a [black] Muslim that I'm sorry for now. I was a zombie then — like all [black] Muslims — I was hypnotized, pointed in a certain direction and told to march. Well, I guess a man's entitled to make a fool of himself if he's ready to pay the cost. It cost me 12 years. That was a bad scene, brother. The sickness and madness of those days — I'm glad to be free of them." -El Hajj Malik El Shabazz.

Farrakhan has denied ordering the assassination of brother Malik El Shabazz but later admitted to having **"helped create the atmosphere"** that led to it. Why all this pressure on Malik? After all, next to Muhammad Ali, Malik El Shabazz was the most influential, well known member of the Nation of Islam and if it wasn't for him, the word of the Nation of Islam wouldn't have been as wide spread as it was. Prior to Malik El Shabazz, the NOI was almost non existent.

"After analyzing these resources, I am convinced that Louis E. Lomax, an industrious African-American journalist who befriended Malcolm X in the late 1950s, had practically solved the riddle of his assassination. He believed that Malcolm X was set up for the assassination by a former friend, John Ali, who was an agent/informer for an intelligence agency. Malcolm X had previously commented that Ali had been responsible for his ouster from the NOI. Ali eventually rose to the position of National Secretary of the NOI. Lomax was later killed in an automobile accident (due to brake failure)."

-Karl Evanzz *The Judas Factor The Plot to Kill Malcolm X* (1992).

It is known through the FOIA that government and law enforcement agencies since The Moorish Science Temple of America, planted infiltrators in almost all of the civil rights movement organizations and some of these agent/informers were highly placed. Their assignments were to report on all of their activities, plans and members, but mostly to create disruption, distrust, confusion and to frighten any supporters. The involvement of the governments COINTELPRO (counter-intelligence program) operation to neutralize El Hajj Malik El through the NOI was due to his upcoming popularity that was unavoidable once he was ousted from the NOI.

Brother Malik's influence among people in general when he came back from Mecca made him bigger than the founders of the NOI and the NOI itself. The only reason we know about Fard Muhammad and Elijah Muhammad is solely due to Malik El Shabazz and his sincerity and honour. Malik El Shabazz was gaining the support of Martin Luther King Jr. to make the struggles of African-Americans an international issue by presenting a petition of human rights violations to the International Court of Justice conference at The Hague. In fact, Malik Shabazz's assassination took place just two weeks before that conference. He was forced to question whether "Black Nationalism" was the correct philosophy. He clearly recognized that using the term Black Nationalist was setting him apart from "true revolutionaries dedicated to overturning the system of exploitation that exists on this earth." Malik El Shabazz found out that he is not negro, black or coloured and changed his tone immediately.

> "Can we sum up the solution to the problems confronting our people as Black Nationalism? If you notice, I haven't been using that expression for several months now."
> - El Hajj Malik El Shabazz

Martin Luther King Jr.

3 April 1968, Mason Temple (Church of God in Christ Headquarters), Memphis, Tennessee

"I've Been to the Mountain Top"
Excerpts

"Thank you very kindly, my friends. As I listened to Ralph Abernathy and his eloquent and generous introduction and then thought about myself, I wondered who he was talking about. It's always good to have your closest friend and associate to say something good about you. And Ralph Abernathy is the best friend that I have in the world."

J. Jackson (L), M.L. King (M) & Ralph Abernathy (R) at Lorraine Motel shortly before King's assassination.

"I recall when Ralph Abernathy, who was once right hand to Dr. Martin Luther King, shortlybefore his demise, appeared on the TODAY Show to "expose King and the SCLC." His big hue and cry was that he was the real hero, and that King could have done nothing had it not been for him. He ranted and raved on national television for about 5 minutes, while a shocked host, and an equally shocked Black viewing audience – and an even more zealously pleased white racist audience – watched. To my mind, this 500 page tome is akin to what I call the Abernathy Syndrome. When you're closer to your death, than you are to your life, and you feel that you've not been given you due, some become bitter and use those last days to heap resentment, instead of joy and pleasure for what they've experienced. Instead they end up leaving behind a legacy of bitterness and acrimony." - Malaak Shabazz

"Overnight Jesse Jackson became a nationally known figure of the civil rights movement. King's wound produced a huge amount of blood and after the ambulance took away his body all that was left was a huge pool of King's blood. Ralph Abernathy in a state of shock grabbed a jar and started scraping up the blood, crying how it was King's blood and precious, "This blood was shed for us." Jesse Jackson also still in shock had by this time made his way to the balcony from where he was hiding down by the pool. Andrew Young remembers seeing Jackson dip his hands in the huge pool of blood and after raising them to the sky wiped them on his shirt, "people freaked out and did strange things ... it was_ it was_ I mean, what do you do in a moment like that"? The main players in the SCLC quickly followed Kind to the hospital leaving Jesse Jackson behind in shock. However, it was the tragedy of King's death that the star of Jesse Jackson was born. Media quickly swarmed the hotel where King had been shot and they quickly focused on the young SCLC member with King's blood all over his shirt. With the rest of the SCLC off at the hospital Jesse became the media spokesman."
- Dean Lucas "Martin Luther King Killed"

Mountain Top excerpts cont'd...

" Something is happening in Memphis; something is happening in our world. And you know, if I were standing at the beginning of time, with the possibility of taking a kind of general and panoramic view of the whole of human history up to now, and the Almighty said to me, "Martin Luther King, which **age** would you like to live in?" Strangely enough, I would turn to the Almighty, and say, "If you allow me to live just a few years in the second half of the 20th century, I will be happy. Now that's a strange statement to make, because the world is all messed up. The nation is sick. Trouble is in the land; confusion all around. That's a strange statement. But I know, somehow, that only when it is dark enough can you see the stars. And I see God working in this period of the twentieth century in a way that men, in some strange way, are responding."

age (n.)

late 13c., "long but indefinite period in human history," from O.Fr. aage (11c., Mod.Fr. âge) "age; life, lifetime, lifespan; maturity," earlier edage, from V.L. *aetaticum from L. aetatem "period of life, age, lifetime, years," from aevum "lifetime, eternity, age," from PIE root *aiw- "vital force, life, long life, eternity" Meaning "time something has lived, particular length or stage of life" is from early 14c.

It was the time of a new age, and Brother Martin Luther King Jr knew that the Baptist time was over, just like El Hajj Malik El Shabazz found out about Black Nationalism and changed his direction. The religious belief held by the oldest and in Europe the most numerous of the Protestant sects, founded by the Wittenberg reformer, Martin Luther. The term *Lutheran* was first used by his opponents during the Leipzig Disputation in 1519, and afterwards became universally prevalent. Luther preferred the designation "Evangelical", and today the usual title of the sect is "Evangelical Lutheran Church". In Germany, where the Lutherans and the Reformed have united (since 1817), the name Lutherans been abandoned, and the state Church is styled the Evangelical or the Evangelical United. Martin Luther King Jr and Martin Luther both changed the worlds they lived in drastically. They were reformers and leaders of their people and died standing up for their people. They were loyal men of faith. Luther the Monk grew up in medieval Germany and the other during the Great Depression. Martin Luther King was a minister in the Baptist Church, one of the strands of Christianity of the Protestant faith Martin Luther is credited with inspiring. Both spent their lives fighting for justice and equality in the eyes of God and their fellow man universally. Both lived lives of controversy and suffered incarceration for standing up for what they believed in with the utmost faith. Both struggled with the laws and doctrines of their time, Luther King worked to eradicate segregation in his Land while Luther nearly brought down the Roman Catholic Church and the Roman Empire.

Mountain Top excerpts cont'd.....

"And also in the human rights revolution, if something isn't done, and done in a hurry, to bring the colored peoples of the world out of their long years of poverty, their long years of hurt and neglect, the whole world is doomed."

http://www.thekingcenter.org/civil-case-king-family-versus-jowers

Coretta Scott King, et al. VS. Loyd Jowers, et al.
IN THE CIRCUIT COURT OF SHELBY COUNTY, TENNESSEE FOR THE THIRTIETH JUDICIAL DISTRICT AT MEMPHIS

CORETTA SCOTT KING, et al,
Plaintiffs,
Vs. Case No. 97242
LOYD JOWERS, et al,
Defendants.

EXCERPT OF PROCEEDINGS
December 8th, 1999

Before the Honorable James E. Swearengen,
Division 4, judge presiding.

DANIEL, DILLINGER, DOMINSKI, RICHBERGER, WEATHERFORD COURT REPORTERS
Suite 2200, One Commerce Square
21 Memphis, Tennessee 38103

APPEARANCES -
For the Plaintiff: DR. WILLIAM PEPPER
Attorney at Law
New York City, New York
For the Defendant:
MR. LEWIS GARRISON
attorney at Law
Memphis, Tennessee

This went on for weeks and weeks and weeks. They spent money, untold sums of money to investigate this case. They concluded that Mr. Ray was the one who pulled the trigger, was the one who did the assassination.

Now, let me say this: After spending several years with this case and talking to many, many witnesses, listening to this trial and taking many depositions, you can't help but wonder about things. You've got to wonder from this standpoint: Would the restaurant owner of a greasy-spoon restaurant and a lone assassin, could they pull away officers from the scene of an assassination? Could they change rooms? Could they put someone up on top of the fire station? A convict and a greasy-spoon restaurant owner, could they do that? You know, when this trial started, there are two people mentioned in this guilty plea who are still living. I talked to them and issued subpoenas for them to be here who are prosecutors to explain you to ladies and gentlemen as to why there wasn't more done to investigate this case. Mr. Ray tried several times, seven, eight, nine times, to get a trial the Court of Appeals, the Supreme Court, never granted it. He was turned down that many times. Why didn't they test the gun? I don't know. It doesn't make sense to me. You know, that would have ended this case if they had tested the gun. There is DNA — they can use means now to test these guns. They could find out if they wanted to. Why wasn't that done? I don't understand.

I've never understood as to why the prosecutors and the Attorney General, if they really wanted to end this case and solve it, why didn't they test the gun. That would have told us whether or not Mr. Ray — that was the gun that did it with his fingerprints on it or was it another gun. It was never done. They fought it and fought it and fought it.

I talked to two prosecutors who agreed to be here to testify, who had subpoenas to be here. The day before yesterday, without you knowing, the Court of Appeals said, no, you can't bring them in. They turned us down again. That's the same thing we've had over and over and over.

Now, ladies and gentlemen, it is ironic in this case that when the extradition proceedings were started against Mr. Ray, that it was to try to extradite him for conspiracy to murder. That was the first thing the United States government tried to extradite Mr. Ray for, was conspiracy to murder.

You know, when you stop and rationalize this case and think, there has to be more it to it than a greasy-spoon restaurant owner and an escaped convict. They could not have arranged these things. They could not have done those things. Mr. Arkin testified here that one hour before the assassination, or a couple hours, there was a man that came in from Washington, sent in here from Washington saying Mr. Redditt has had a threat on his life and you've got to go get him. Could a greasy-spoon operator and escaped convict arrange for that? You know that's not the case. And I do, too. Anyone who can think knows better than that. Mr. Arkin also said there were officers from the United States government in his office. Why were they here? What were they doing here? They were sent here by the United States government.

Now, ladies and gentlemen, we've had problems with race in Memphis, and I'm sorry to say that I must talk about it to some extent. It has been said by a person who was very knowledgeable that we have the most serious racial divisions in Memphis of any city in this nation, and that's bad, that's terrible. We've got to live together and learn to live together and to know that we are all bothers and sisters. It shouldn't be this way. It shouldn't be we should have this type racism and the type problems we have.

In this case you have the opportunity to speak. You'll speak in your verdict in case that will either say one of two things: That we know that there was a conspiracy here, we know that they didn't intend for Dr. King to go to Washington to march, and we know that the United States government, the FBI and the Memphis Police Department and other government agencies along with Mr. Liberto and Mr. Earl Clark and Mr. James Earl Ray were involved in this case, and that's the type verdict that I would ask you to consider.

You told me at the beginning you weren't afraid to let the chips fall where they may. I gather from that that you are not afraid of the United States government. You are not afraid of the Memphis Police Department. If they are liable, you are going to say they are. Am I correct? Isn't that what we agreed to?

I think the testimony here that you've heard and the proof that you've heard indicates clearly there is more than just Mr. Jowers involved. He was a small-time greasy-spoon cafe operator who played a very small significant part in this case, if anything. If you will study over the reports I've provided for you and the exhibits, think about all the testimony that has been given here and what really happened, ladies and gentlemen, your verdict would have to be that the United States government, the FBI, the Memphis Police Department and others were involved in this conspiracy to murder Dr. King.

It is a shameful, terrible thing that happened here in Memphis. I'm sorry and apologize to Mr. King that it did, but think about it. It is a very serious matter. You'll never have a more serious opportunity to sit on a jury than this where the issues are more serious than this. Whatever you say will be recorded in history, and this will be it. We expect this case to end after this. It has been going on for years, but we think it is going to end with your decision in this case.

Please give it serious consideration and please think about a judgment against others besides Mr. Jowers. He played a very small part, you know he did, in this case. Think about the other part that Mr. Ray played, Mr. Liberto played. You've got testimony here from a witness that is un-contradicted saying that Mr. Liberto told me he had Martin Luther King assassinated. Go over it. Think about it. Read over it. There is only one thing to do, that's to say that we the jury find that the United States government, FBI, State of Tennessee, Mr. Liberto, Mr. James Earl Ray, they were all involved in a conspiracy to murder Dr. Martin Luther King. That's the only decision can you make.

Thank you.

Decision:

THE COURT: I understand the jury has reached a verdict. I'm going to bring them out. They've indicated that they want a picture of themselves. So I'm authorizing this gentleman to take one picture. He is going to make sure there are no additional copies. I'll have copies made of them and send them to the jurors.

THE COURT: All right, ladies and gentlemen. I understand you reached a verdict. Is that correct?

THE JURY: Yes (In unison).

THE COURT: May I have that verdict.

THE COURT: I have authorized this gentleman here to take one picture of you which I'm going to have developed and make copies and send to you as I promised. Okay. All right, ladies and gentlemen. Let me ask you, do all of you agree with this verdict?

THE JURY: Yes (In unison).

THE COURT: In answer to the question did Lloyd Jowers participate in a conspiracy to do harm to Dr. Martin Luther King, your answer is yes. **Do you also find that others, including governmental agencies, were parties to this conspiracy as alleged by the defendant? Your answer to that one is also yes.** And the total amount of damages you find for the plaintiffs entitled to is one hundred dollars. Is that your verdict?

THE JURY: Yes (In unison).

"This historic trial was so ignored by the media that, apart from the courtroom participants, I was the only person who attended it from beginning to end. What I experienced in that courtroom ranged from inspiration at the courage of the Kings, their lawyer-investigator <u>William F. Pepper</u>, and the witnesses, to amazement at the government's carefully interwoven plot to kill Dr. King. The seriousness with which US intelligence agencies planned the murder of Martin Luther King, Jr. speaks eloquently of the threat King and <u>nonviolence</u> represented to the powers that be in the spring of 1968. " - Jim Douglass

"There is abundant evidence of a major high level conspiracy in the assassination of my husband, Martin Luther King, Jr... the conspiracy of the Mafia, local, state and federal government agencies, were deeply involved in the assassination of my husband. The jury also affirmed overwhelming evidence that identified someone else, not James Earl Ray, as the shooter, and that Mr. Ray was set up to take the blame." Coretta Scott King

Mountain Top excerpts cont'd

"You know, whenever Pharaoh wanted to prolong the period of slavery in Egypt, he had a favorite, favorite formula for doing it. What was that? He kept the slaves fighting among themselves. But whenever the slaves get together, something happens in Pharaoh's court, and he cannot hold the slaves in slavery. When the slaves get together, that's the beginning of getting out of slavery. Now let us maintain unity....We have an injunction and we're going into court tomorrow morning to fight this illegal, unconstitutional injunction. But somewhere I read of the freedom of assembly. Somewhere I read of the freedom of speech. Somewhere I read of the freedom of press. Somewhere I read that the greatness of America is the right to protest for right."

August, 28th, 1963, Dr. Martin Luther King Jr.'s famous I have a dream speech, was not about black and white children playing together, and black men and white men etc.. Its was about enforcing the Constitution for the United States of America Republic. The *I Have a Dream* speech was the early sign to El Hajj Malik El Shabazz that he had a Constitutional ally for the fight against those against Human Rights or Nationality and Birthrights. In 1964 was when El Hajj left the NOI and met Dr. King.

"In the last years of their lives, they were starting to move toward one another," says David Howard-Pitney, who recounted the Capitol Hill meeting in his book "Martin Luther King, Jr., Malcolm X, and the Civil Rights Struggle of the 1950s and 1960s."

"While Malcolm is moderating from his earlier position, King is becoming more militant," Pitney says. Malcolm X was reaching out to King even before he broke away from the Nation of Islam and embraced Sunni Islam after a pilgrimage to Mecca, says Andrew Young, a member of King's inner circle at the Southern Christian Leadership Conference, the civil rights group King headed. " Even before his trip to Mecca, Malcolm used to come by the SCLC's office," Young says. "Unfortunately, Dr. King was never there when he came." - John Blake CNN

Mountaintop excerpts cont'd

"And then I got into Memphis. And some began to say the threats, or talk about the threats that were out. What would happen to me from some of our sick white brothers? Well, I don't know what will happen now. We've got some difficult days ahead. But it really doesn't matter with me now, because I've been to the mountaintop. And I don't mind.

Like anybody, I would like to live a long life. Longevity has its place. But I'm not concerned about that now. I just want to do God's will. And He's allowed me to go up to the mountain. And I've looked over. And I've seen the Promised Land. I may not get there with you. But I want you to know tonight, that we, as a people, will get to the promised land! And so I'm happy, tonight. I'm not worried about anything. I'm not fearing any man! Mine eyes have seen the glory of the coming of the Lord!!"

On Feb. 21, 1965, El Hajj Malik El Shabazz was killed by gunfire and on April 4, 1968 Dr. Martin Luther King Jr was killed by gunfire, and it is common knowledge they were assassinated as part of the biggest conspiracy against the liberation and salvation of Asiatics in the Americas and of the World. On March 23, 1964, Elijah Muhammad told Boston minister Louis X (later known as <u>Louis Farrakhan</u>) that "hypocrites like Malcolm should have their heads cut off." **On June 8, a man called Malcolm X's home and told Betty Shabazz to "tell him he's as good as dead."**

What must also be looked at is the famous *I've Been to the Mountaintop*.

" Pyramids completed by capstones, which like *mountaintops* are the symbolic locale of wisdom." - Seven Star Hand "Here is more Light"

"Freemasonic lore and symbols have been traced to ancient Egypt and Phoenicia. Yet, despite all the books and articles exploring Freemasonry published over the last hundred years, there is one area that has not received attention. It concerns Freemasonry's debt to Islamic mysticism and a shadowy tradition connecting the Masons with the Moors of North Africa. Moor is the classical name in Europe of the Muslim people of North Africa. In Spain, where Muslims ruled for over five hundred years, Arabs are still called Moros. The term "Moor" came to be synonymous with "Muslim" in many contexts, for example the Muslim communities in the Philippines are known to this day as Moros. The Supreme Wisdom of the Moors, much of it derived from ancient Egypt, has come to be known as "Moorish Science".

The Moors provided the vital link between ancient and modern civilization. The light of knowledge which illuminated the Moorish lands of Spain and Sicily was instrumental in dispelling the gloom of ignorance that enveloped mediaeval Europe."- MEHMET SABEHEDDIN

The document on which the Great Seal first appeared (Sept. 16, 1782) concludes as follows:

"In Testimony whereof we have caused these our Letters to be made patent and the Great Seal of the United States of America to be thereunto affixed. Witness His Excellency John Hanson President of the United States in Congress assembled the sixteenth day of September in the Year of our Lord one thousand seven hundred and Eighty two, And of our **Sovereignty & Independence**."

This ubiquitous image is most often referred to as the **all seeing eye** or "**eye of providence.**" The all seeing eye, usually depicted in the sky looking out upon the earth, is an ancient symbol of the sun, and historically has been used as a symbol of omniscience. In the Library of Congress, the symbol of the Eye is called Allah. The idea of the solar eye comes to us from Kemet. We equated the eye with the deity Heru, the human eye in its ability to perceive light was viewed as a miniature sun.

The use of the eye emblem to represent God was quite common in the Renaissance when the Moors were teaching the inepts of Europe; often, the **eye** would be enclosed within a triangle representing the triune godhead. The best place to see the horizon is from a mountain top. Dr King Jr. was speaking in code to anyone who was willing to take of their dogma blinders. He was telling us that he saw the promise land by knowing about human rights not civil rights. He knew there was a bigger perspective, and once the establishment finds out, that someone so popular, with influence internationally, is about to expose the negro black coloured subjugated status conspiracy. They must be exterminated. This is why Drew Ali warned the Moors, if you don't do anything else, declare your nationality. Dr. King Jr., like El hajj, knew they were going to be assassinated. Noble Drew Ali knew as well, and the pattern ever since Noble Drew Ali, was to get so close to the top man, that it will be so easy to get rid of him. El Hajj had Louis X, Brother Martin Jr had messy Jesse and Ralph Abernathy. The Promise Land that Dr. King Jr. was referring to was the North Gate. Dr. King Jr. either had to be a mason, or, through brother El Hajj, found out about Nationality and Birthrights. Moors know that there is an agitation that grows when you find out about the Law, and that you've denied it to yourself for so long. There's a frustration that comes about from doing diligent study, that the information is so easily accessible, why aren't the leaders of the "black" nation talking about it? Why are there eye brows raised and sudden deaths of leaders when the talks of rights over privileges arise? Brother King and Shabazz are great examples of not being caught up in the physical, and doing what you can to redeem the race spiritually, when you realize the odds you are up against your own trying to assassinate you. And in the tone of Noble Drew Ali, they did the same. Just put the information out all at once in code, and may Allah guide and protect you.

> "Where is the memorial for all the African Americans who have been killed, raped and lynched in this country"
> -Dr. Velu Annamalai

Muhammad Ali

At a press conference the day after the Liston fight, Muhammad Ali announced his allegiance to the Nation of Islam and shared with the world his new name. This turnabout dismayed Malcolm and his wife, Betty Shabazz because remember all the denunciations of Ali before the fight, the hysteria about how he would "bring disgrace to the Nation of Islam," and so on.

"They were breaking their necks, trying to get close to the heavyweight champion. Muhammad Ali" - Betty Shabazz

Originally the name was Cassius X. The rejection of "Clay" horrified his parents, especially his father, whose name had been devalued in every sense of the word.

"The boxer's father, Cassius Clay Sr., was very proud of the Clay name. It also hurt the Sr. Clay deeply when Cassius Jr. denounced the name and became known as Muhammad Ali. It broke a tradition and ignored a source of pride that the Sr. Clay held dear. At first when the young Clay changed his name, it led to bitter arguments and a period of time when the father and son did not speak. Later, Sr. accepted his son's decision, but never forgave him for the denouncing of the Clay heritage. " - Cassius Clay by Troy R. Kinunen

With his conversion to Islam, Clay adopted a more traditional name. The changing of the name was thought by some to be a public denouncing of his family name and heritage. In which case it was, because from a Law perspective, Clay is a European name and Cassius was an Asiatic. The traits associated with the original Cassius Marcellus Clay, are all traits that can be labeled with the very act of Clay changing his name and converting to Islam. With the name change, Cassius X began his journey of fighting the establishment and adhering to progressive ideals and values he was beginning to experience by his association with the NOI. The very act of fighting the establishment, questioning authority, and challenging current social norms, were the same traits of his father, who supported the slave brand Clay. Speaking to 5,000 followers at the annual Nation of Islam convention, Elijah Muhammad joyously announced that "Clay whipped a much tougher man and came through the bout unscarred because he ha:

accepted Muhammad as the messenger of Allah." In the Nation of Islam one would receive an "original name" – i.e. an Arabic ONLY AFTER the "prophetic" founder Master Fard Muhammad returned from wherever it was he had gone. Thus, even after his years of dedicated service, Malcolm remained merely Malcolm X. But the Nation of Islam, "bendable" as it was, made an exception for an unschooled 22-year-old in a "filthy" profession. On a March 6 1964 in a radio broadcast from Chicago, Elijah Muhammad gave the young boxer his new name, Muhammad Ali from Cassius X and by aligning himself with the Nation of Islam at that time made him fit for controversy, turning the outspoken but popular champion into one of that era's most recognizable and controversial up and coming "black Muslim" figures. Why did Elijah suddenly step in and upgrade the name change from Cassius X to Muhammad Ali, without the permission of Fard Muhammad?

"My conscience wont let me shoot my brother or some darker people, or some poor hungry people in the mud for big powerful America, and shoot them for what? They never called me nigger, they never lynched me, they never put dogs on me, they never robbed me of my NATIONALITY.. How am I going to shoot those poor people? Just take me to jail.."

-Muhammad Ali

Muhammad Ali was not the ONLY Asiatic in America against the Vietnam War. Many people refused to go to war when drafted. Muhammad Ali was the only one with the most to lose. Muhammad Ali was already an icon and public figure and the NOI heads saw this as an amazing opportunity to catapult themselves into the future as the organization connected to the landmark decision of this so called black man "dodging the democracy military draft". The NOI eyes lit up, because they too were shown the promise Land of the North Gate and that NATIONALITY was and is the order of the day especially dis-guised to the ignorant masses as something different to what Noble Drew Ali brought and taught.

Canadian boxing legend George Chuvalo went 15 rounds with Muhammad Ali at Maple Leaf Gardens in Toronto on March 29, 1966 in a bout billed as "a heavyweight showdown." Chuvalo hung with Ali late into the fight but the champ was too quick for the Canadian. Ali won by unanimous decision.

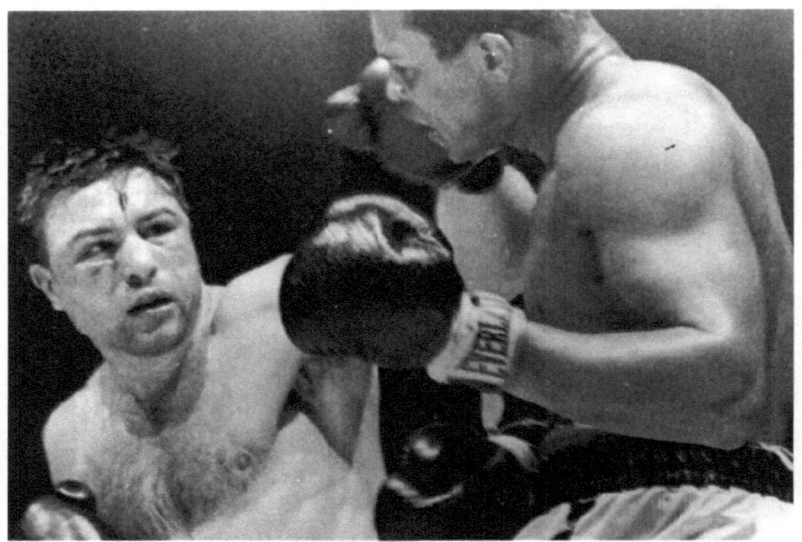

Chuvalo was inducted into the World Boxing Hall of Fame in 1997 and was made a Member of the Order of Canada in 1998.

To recap, 1963, Clay defeated British heavyweight champion Henry Cooper and set his sights on world champion Sonny Liston. Clay won when Liston failed to answer the bell for the seventh round. The next day, he held a news conference, announcing his conversion to Islam and adopting the name Cassius X, which soon to be Muhammad Ali. Many refused to even use his newly adopted name. The Justice Department pursued Ali for alleged draft evasion after he failed to report for induction into the United States military on religious grounds when it was really due to his proclaiming his Nationality. In the middle of this controversy, Ali beat challenger Ernie Terrell -- who continued to refer to Ali as "Clay'. Before and during the fight, Ali taunting him with, "What's my name?" during their bout. In 1967, Ali was convicted of draft evasion and stripped of his titles, boxing licenses and passport.

"I have searched my conscience and I find I cannot be true to my belief in my religion by accepting such a call. ... If justice prevails, if my Constitutional rights are upheld, I will be forced to go neither to the Army nor jail. In the end I am confident that justice will come my way for the truth must eventually prevail." - Muhammad Ali

Ali spent the next three years free, as Ali, while his conviction as CLAY was on appeal; Keep in mind this is 2 years after El Hajj is assassinated and the new face of the NOI was Muhammad Ali, who lectured at universities and Muslim gatherings and gained constitutional support as antiwar sentiment increased. Muhammad Ali fought Jerry Quarry in 1970, why not as Cassius Clay? His appeal would reach the Supreme Court in 1971. In Clay v. United States, the Court ruled 8-0 that Ali met the three standards for conscientious objector status: that he opposed war in any form, that his beliefs were based on religious teaching and that his objection was sincere. His conviction was reversed.

"Shortly after the Quarry fight, theNew York State Supreme Court ruled that Ali had been unjustly denied a boxing license. Once again able to fight in New York, he fought Oscar Bonavena at Madison Square Garden in December 1970. Ali and Frazier met in the ring on March 8, 1971, at Madison Square Garden. The fight, known as "The Fight of the Century," was one of the most eagerly anticipated bouts of all time and remains one of the most famous. "

Saying all that to stress the point that in 1964, the boxer was renamed Muhammad Ali. Two days later, Malcolm X announced that he had left the NOI. He soon created two new organizations, the Muslim Mosque, Inc., designed for former NOI members as a spiritually-based group, and the secular-oriented Organization of Afro-American Unity This was when the transition of power went from Malcolm X to Muhammad Ali because of the power in a free national name. And this was the TRUTH that, then Malcolm X found out and was verified with Cassius X, correcting his name, to Ali.

"You know your slogan – 'The white man is a devil, the white devils' – that's not right. You can't live in this world hating people," - Sugar Ray Robinson quote Jack Cashill Sucker Punch

Ernesto "Che" Guevera

In 1960 Che Guevara visited China and the Soviet Union. On his return he wrote two books Guerrilla Warfare and Reminiscences of the Cuban Revolutionary War. In December 1964, when Cuban leader Ernesto Che Guevara came to New York to address the UN, El Hajj Malik El Shabazz invited him to come to the Audubon Ballroom to speak to a meeting of the OAAU [Organization of Afro-American Unity].

Che later concluded that "security conditions are not good for my participation in this meeting. Receive the warm salutations of the Cuban people and especially those of Fidel, who remembers enthusiastically his visit to Harlem a few years ago. United we will win."

Che had spoken before the United Nations two days earlier. In that speech he had championed one of the anti-imperialist struggles El Hajj Malik El Shabazz also felt very deeply about: the liberation struggle in the Congo. In June 1960, after nearly a century of incredibly bloody and exploitative Belgian rule, the Congolese people had won their independence and established a government led by the Great Prime Minister Patrice Lumumba. And we know what happed to Brother Lamumba. Under United Nations cover, they engineered a coup against Lumumba in September 1960 and his brutal murder in January 1961 and no one was surprised when fingers started pointing at the CIA. A Senate investigation of CIA assassinations 14 years later claimed the agency was not behind the hit, as usual, but truth needs no Senate investigation. Today, new evidence suggests Belgium, Congo's former colonialist ruler, was the mastermind. According to *The Assassination of Lumumba*, by sociologist Ludo de Witte, Belgian operatives directed and carried out the murder, and even helped dispose of the body. Washington and Brussels immediately organized to destroy the Lumumba government and replace it with a regime they were confident would protect imperialism's vast copper and other mineral holdings. Back to Brother Che...

Che pointed out to the General Assembly—and above all, from that podium, to the working people of the world—that Washington and other imperialist powers had "used the name of the United Nations to commit the murder of Lumumba" and of thousands of Congolese villagers. "All free men of the world must be prepared to avenge the crime of the Congo.

Che left straight from New York in mid-December for a three-month tour of Africa, there, he met with leaders of the Lumumba forces, of governments on the continent who supported the Congolese anti-imperialist rebels, and of national liberation movements in Angola and other countries then still under the boot of Portuguese rule. In 1965 Che was in the Congo, leading a column of Cuban internationalist volunteers who helped arm and train the pro-Lumumba forces. After a brief return to Cuba for additional training and preparations, Che in late 1966 left for Bolivia.

He refused to talk about what he had done in Africa although, when I said we'd been told he had a ten thousand-man guerrilla force, but that his African soldiers were a disaster, he laughed sadly and said, "If I'd really had ten thousand guerrillas it would have been different. But you are right, you know - the Africans were very, very bad soldiers. Che expressed surprise that I knew so much about him, and about Cuba. "You are not a Bolivian," he said.

"No, I am not. Where do you think I am from?"

"You could be a Puerto Rican or a Cuban. Whoever you are, by the sorts of questions you've been asking I believe that you work for the intelligence service of the United States."

"You are right, Comandante," I said. "I am a Cuban. I was a member of the 2506 Brigade. In fact, I was a member of the infiltration teams that operated inside Cuba before the invasion at the Bay of Pigs."

"What's your name?"

"Felix. Just Felix, Comandante." I wanted to say more, but I didn't dare. There was still a slim possibility that he might get out of this alive, and I didn't want my identity to escape with him.

"Ha," Che answered. Nothing more. I don't know what he was thinking at the moment and I never asked.

We started to talk about the Cuban economy once again when we were interrupted by shots, followed by the sounds of a body falling to the floor. Aniceto had been executed in the adjoining room. Che stopped talking. He did not say anything about the shooting, but his face reflected sadness and he shook his head slowly from left to right several times.

Perhaps it was in that instant that he realized that he, too, was doomed, even though I did not tell him so until just before 1 P.M.

I had been putting off the inevitable, shuttling between Che's room and the table where I was photographing his documents. I was taking pictures of his diary when the village schoolteacher arrived.

"Mi Capitan?"

I looked up from my work. "Yes?"

"When are you going to shoot him?"

That caught my attention. "Why are you asking me that?" I asked.

"Because the radio is already reporting that he is dead from combat wounds."

The Bolivians were taking no chances. That radio report sealed Che's fate. I went down the hill, into the schoolhouse and looked Che in the face. "Comandante, " I said, "I have done everything in my power, but orders have come from the Supreme Bolivian Command..." - Felix I Rodriguez Shadow Warrior

On April 20, 1976, the CIA agent Felix I Rodriguez, who had orchestrated the hunt for Che Guevara in Bolivia, retired. By his own account Rodriguez's most magnificent moment came when he lifted off in a helicopter from La Higuera, Bolivia, on October 9, 1967, with Che Guevara's body lashed to the right skid. "On my wrist was his steel Rolex GMT Master with its red-and-blue bezel," he recounted. "In my breast pocket, wrapped in paper from my loose-leaf notebook, was the partially smoked tobacco from his last pipe."

Many have sold out and became agents in the attempt to bury the National perspectives that Noble Drew Ali brought and taught to ALL the Nations. The Moorish Divine and National Movement leaders organization was the foundation of secret operatives and puppets being used by the democracy to destabilize Republic mindsets. Through covert tactics the democracy has went around the world implementing the Treaty of Verona and Spanish Inquisition practices of the past in the face of the people. The people have missed the mark with regard to pointing out who the real enemy is. Che, Martin, El Hajj, Khallid Muhammad, Patrice Lamumba and the list goes on, were all assassinated by their own, be cause their own had no honour in them. Their own brothers and sisters sided with the colonial powers to get a piece of the booty. Some of the agents get used and abused, while some others live in the lap of luxury for the rest of their lives. Do not be fooled. Do your own due diligence, and play detective all the time. Always have your eyes open and never forget that we can not continue to speak about new world order conspiracies without addressing the negro black coloured addiction and the conspiracy that caused negro black coloured people to not know they are Moors.

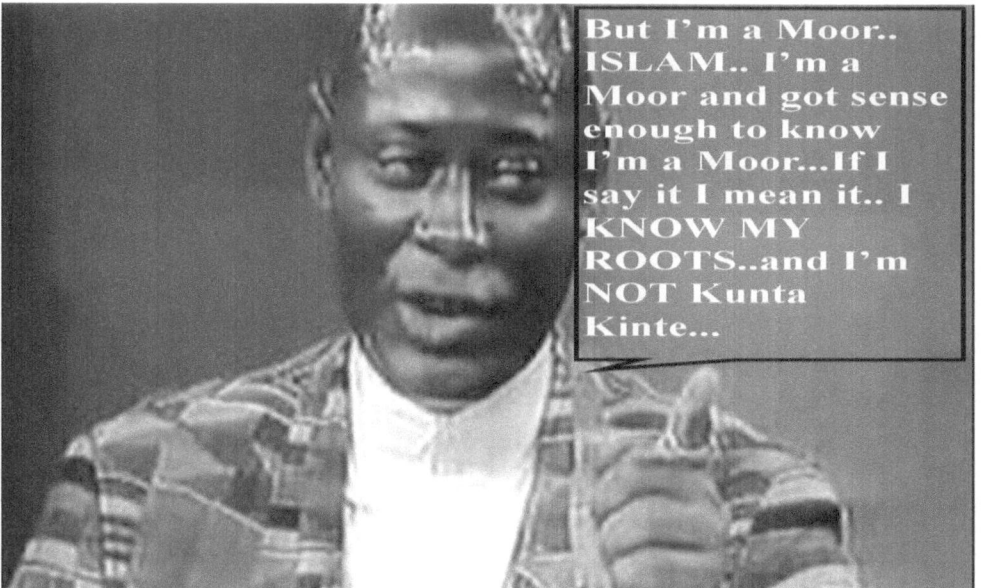

Yasiin Bey

At a performance last August, the deliberate and sharply dressed emcee, who is also well known as an actor, announced his "official transition" to a huge audience gathered in the parking lot of a popular pub and pizzeria in Anchorage, Alaska: "My professional name will be my chosen and my legal name, which is Yasiin Bey. ... And I don't want to have to wait for it to be in *Source* or *Vibe* or someplace. I figure, we're all here. We can see each other." And then he spelled it out for them: "Y-A-S-I-I-N, first name. Last name: B-E-Y." When a few Alaskans made some disapproving noises, Bey responded, "I understand. I understand." Cradling his signature bright red, vintage-style microphone, he then tried to make it clear he knew exactly what, and exactly whom, he was giving up. "No one has a more close relationship to Mos Def than me. I know that guy. *Really good.*"

"Yasiin" is an Arabic word and Yasiin Bey is Muslim, arguably the most prominent pop-cultural Muslim figure since Muhammad Ali, a hero of Bey's, who went through his own series of name changeswhen entering the Nation of Islam under the wings of Malcolm X in the mid-60s. Bey is either a convert from his mother's Christianity and the church that shapes his earliest memories of music, or he's what's often referred to as a "revert" to the Islam of his father, Abdul Rahman, or Abi. ("Umi" and "abi" are Arabic words that mean "mother" and "father," respectively.)

As Bey's brother, also Abdul Rahman, told me, "Everybody's born Muslim." In Islam, this fact is contained in the idea of *fitrah*, that every child possesses the innate understanding of the unity of God. It is our original nature. Coming to terms with that is, in part, simply what the revert does. Bey, however, seems to have come into his Islam through music. His father's deeper impact notwithstanding, his conversion can be attributed largely to the influence of the pioneering hip-hop group A Tribe Called Quest. And though members of the group would not credit themselves with Bey's becoming a Muslim, they were there when it happened—"*so* there," deejay Ali Shaheed Muhammad told me. Bey declared himself a Muslim at Battery Recording Studios on 25th Street in New York City surrounded by members of Tribe during the making of their 1996 album *Beats, Rhymes and Life.* - Scott Korb

Chief Mustafa Malik Ang-El (Jeff Fort)

In the name of Almighty God Allah. The most Gracious and most Merciful. ISLAM my brother Kudjo El from the M.S.T.A in Canada. I hope that when this letter reaches you, you're in the best of health and spirit.

" That naught is naught; that power is but illusion; that Heaven and Earth and Hell are not above, around, below, but in; which in the lights of night become naught. And Allah is All"

I wanted to inform you that I received the book that you sent and to express my appreciation. It's easy to exercise your body. But it is also imperative to exercise your mind. That is why it's always a pleasure to receive good literature to exercise my mind.

" The blessing, O Man, of thy external part is health, vigor and proportion. The greatest of these is health. What health is to the body even that is honesty to the soul".

Again I want to thank you for the book. Until next time.

Chief Mustafa Malik Ang-El

Peace and Love

El Rukn is an Arabic term that refers to "foundation". Law enforcement didn't relent despite the name change from Blackstone Rangers. Prosecutors, to make an example out of the honourable street disciple Chief Malik El, tried out their new "war on drugs" policies on El Rukns and Chief Malik was sent to prison in 1983. The U.S Democracy corporation contended that they heard Chief Malik on tape belittle NOI Minister Louis Farrakhan for taking money from Muammar Muhammad Abu Minyar al-Gaddafi . Farrakhan had received a $5 million loan from Gaddafi to start a line of black personal care products. The Nation of Islam's international headquarters, purchased 40 years ago with a $3 million loan from Gadhafi .

During the 1960's, then Jeff Fort, earned the nickname Angel for his ability to solve disputes and form alliances between the Rangers and other gangs, By the mid 1960's Fort assembled a coalition of 21 Gangs with about 5,000 members. He organized the coalition under a governing body. The Rangers were involved in community and political activism. Fort converted to ISLAMISM and joined the MSTA in 1976. The Stones were then renamed the El Rukn Tribe of the Moorish Science Temple. In 1987 Chief Malik El was falsely tried and convicted for conspiring with Libya . The question then arises how come Farrakhan is still free when he openly conspired and supported Gaddafi but Chief Malik El is serving 100 plus years in ADX Florence super-max prison? Considering that the U.S Cointelpro had a hand in Chief being sent to prison, they must have a hand in Farrakhan not being in prison.

One of the young masters, Bro Aseer the Duke of Tiers teaches us that Moorish Science and the essence of it has weaved its way into Hip Hop culture and that the world famous hairstyle of the Golden era of Hip Hop, the cameo, as worn by Kid, Big Daddy Kane, and many other Emcees of that era, is a hair fez. So even Hip Hop Emcees of the Golden Era were subconsciously teaching us, directly and indirectly about our Moorish Culture. Keep in mind that the music of that era was also very conscious and was nothing compared to the garbage we hear RAPPERS coming out with in these times. Even some of our favorite Emcees were plenipotentiaries of the Prophet Noble Drew Ali. ISLAM

Visual Alchemy

Here is a picture of Father Divine standing at the table like the Noble Prophet Drew Ali. Notice Father Divine is wearing the same striped style tie as the Noble Prophet.

Sweet Daddy Grace holding the scepter of power copying the frontispiece of Thomas Hobbes <u>Leviathan</u>, depicting the Sovereign as a massive body wielding a <u>sword</u> and <u>crozier</u> and composed of many individual people. The idea of Sovereignty and "God" or Allah being in man, was resurrected in America by Prophet Noble Drew Ali.

Elijah Muhammad and Fruits of Islam in fezzes. As well Jabir Herbert Muhammad, son of Nation of Islam leader Elijah Muhammad and long time manager of boxing legend Muhammad Ali.

Nation of Islam National Spokesman Louis Farrakhan wearing the F.O.I. fez.

The Moors and Christians will be parading once again during their yearly fiesta through the streets of Orihuela. The Fiesta de la Reconquista commemorates the battles for control of the land between the Moors and Christians.

Bibliography, website-ography, dvd-ography

Abdelwahid, Mustafa. *Duse Mohamed Ali*. Trenton, NJ: The Red Sea Press, Inc, 2011.

"American Moors: Our True Identity." *Pointing Bird*. n.d. http://pointingbird.tripod.com/lostfeatherintl/id64.htm (accessed July 27, 2014).

Bey, C.M. *Clock of Destiny Vol. 1*. Clock of Destiny International Order of the Great Seal, n.d.

Bey, Hannibal, interview by Sabir Bey. "Civil Alert Radio." *Moor Insight: Cleaning Out Part II*. (August 10, 2012).

Bey, Hannibal, interview by Sabir Bey. "Civil Alert Radio." *Moor Insight: Cleaning Out the Closet Part I*. (2012).

Bro. Edwards El, R. et. al. *The Muqarrabeen File Book 1 Complete*. SMD Media Group, 2008.

Clock of Destiny. *Clock of Destity*. n.d. http://www.clockofdestiny.com/.

Evanzz, Karl. *The Judas Factor: The Plot To Kill Malcolm X*. New York: Thunder Mouth , 1993.

Finley. Stephen C., Alexander, Torin. *African American Religious Cultures*. Edited by Anthony B. Pinn. 2 vols. Santa Barbara, CA: ABC-CLIO, 2009.

Jackson, John G and Huggins, Willis N. *A Guide to Studies in African History: Directive Lists for Schools and Clubs*. Federation of History Clubs, 1934.

KING vs. JOWERS. 97242-4 T.D. (Supreme Court of Tennessee, December 13, 1999).

Kinunen, Troy R. "Cassius Clay: The Early Years 1954-60. A Study of the Man Through His Memorabilia. ." *MERS: Memorabilia Evaluation & Research Services* (MERS: Memorabilia Evaluation & Research Services), 2006.

Moorishciviletter.net. *Moorishciviletter.net.* n.d. http://Moorishciviletter.net.

R.V. Bey Publications. *R.V. Bey Publications.* n.d. http://rvbeypublications.com.

The Colonial Press. *Moorish Literature.* New York: The Colonial Press, 1901.

U.S. Government. "King Alfred Plan." U.S. Federal Government, 1984.

Other Titles from Califa Media Publishing ™

Moorish Children's Guide to History and Culture

Moorish Jewels: Emerald Ed

Moors in America

Moslem Girls' Training Guide a.k.a. The Sisters' Auxiliary Handbook

Nationality, the Order of the Day

Noble Drew Ali Plenipotentiaries

Official Proclamation of Real Moorish American Nationality

Well, Come to Klanada

Califa Uhuru Series

Vol. 1: Holy Koran of the Moorish Holy Temple of Science, Circle 7

Vol. 2: "I'm Going to Repeat Myself.": A Collection of Artifacts Authored by Noble Prophet Drew Ali and the M.S.T. of A.

Vol. 3: Mysteries of the Silent Brotherhood of the East a.ka. The Red Book, a.k.a. Sincerity

Vol. 4: Califa Uhuru; A Collection of Literature from the Moorish Science Temple of America

www.ingramcontent.com/pod-product-compliance
Lightning Source LLC
Chambersburg PA
CBHW030200100526
44592CB00009B/366